Jim Bouchard
is available for Corporate
& Public Events, Conventions,
Executive Training & Retreats.

For more information call
800-786-8502

On the web:
www.JimBouchard.org

Dynamic Components of Personal POWER

Jim Bouchard

Success...The Black Belt Way!

First Edition 2007

San Chi Publishing
Brunswick, Maine

The Dynamic Components of Personal Power
by Jim Bouchard

Published and distributed in the United States by San Chi Publishing
10 Jordan Avenue, Brunswick, Maine, USA
www.SanChi.biz
Linda Pritchard, Editor

First Edition 2007
Printed in the United States of America

ISBN Softcover edition: 978-0-6151-5916-4

Library of Congress Control Number: 2007906116

Gratitude...

This project was possible only through the support, encouragement and cooperation of many treasured friends, family and colleagues.

It's impossible to acknowledge everyone who made this book possible. It's best to simply thank all the wonderful teachers and coaches I've had throughout my career so far, Grandmaster Mark Shuey and Dr. Yang, Jwing-Ming stand out among them. Many others made important contributions to my understanding of life and power. It's also appropriate to thank all my students; you've been my sounding board as I've organized and developed this philosophy.

Very special thanks to Linda Pritchard for her skillful editing, encouraging dialogue, and candid review.

Very special thanks to the Dynamic Components team led by Steve Wallace who saw greater potential in my work and helped me see over the horizon.

Very special thanks to a group of friends I rely on to keep me focused on higher ground: Paul Clark, Dave Melville, Smokey Hicks, Lori Blackburn, Ed Pritchard, Ken Ryan and Jim Cusano. I'm thankful for your friendship in good times and your support through tough times.

Very special thanks to Alexandra Armstrong, my partner in life and business, who has always provided unwavering support in the face of every adversity and who helped me believe in the importance and validity of my work.

Finally, very special thanks to Don Lonsway for spending much of his adult life trying to convince me to become a teacher; I hope you feel that your time was well spent!

Top notch speaker, motivator, and educator rolled into one! I have worked with Jim over the past three months and by far, what he has to offer to my clients, has been exceptional.

Jim's four-part workshops on creating and maintaining personal power, culminating with developing an entrepreneurial edge, have been some of the best attended, highest rated workshops over the past two-years!

Jim doesn't just "give people information," he motivates them to use the information given and make themselves and those around them better! *I highly recommend Jim to anyone that wants to grow their employee base and or motivate themselves to reach the next level.*

Steve Wallace
Southern Midcoast Chamber of Commerce
and Director of Brunswick Naval Air Station BRAC Transition Team

Thank you for the outstanding program you provided to Oakhurst Dairy on "Respect in the Workplace". *Both our executive and middle management level staff members enjoyed it so much we now wish to invite you to present both segments of the program to all our employees this spring...*

You have my sincere gratitude for a job well done as indicated by the very complimentary evaluations you received. We now have a new Code of Ethics and Respect that went into place earlier this week. Much of the credit for this new document come as a direct result of all the discussion in the senior leadership team meeting following your program.

Thanks again, Jim. Simple, yet excellent. That's how we describe your program!

Joe Hyatt
Vice-President, Human Resources
Oakhurst Dairy

I want to sincerely thank you for the time you spent with us...your presentation was just what was needed. I compliment you on the content and the method you presented your message on "Dynamic Components of Personal Power". ...selfishly more importantly the philosophy you presented of connecting discipline, time, spirit/health, focus, balance, and motivation in triangles with their interdependency helps give a visual structure to what you practice and teach.

The Alion staff...gained invaluable insight as to how ones spirit/heart affects development of healthy living; how strong spirit and mind leads to strong bodies, which in turn leads to a greater sense of confidence. *Having our heart in the right state will create a positive outlook (mind) of ones situation, which will help the body in developing good heath habits. All of which make the person a better contributor to their family, their co-workers and employer and their community in general.*

Lee Fournier
Assistant Vice-President, Division Manager
Alion Science & Technology

Contents

Introduction

I make two promises to all my martial arts students, and only two, assuming you're willing to do what it takes to make it to *Black Belt.* First, within the scope of your talents and abilities, you can do anything you want to do with your life. Second, you'll learn how to recognize and develop your talents and abilities.

To a martial artist, the *Black Belt* is the ultimate symbol of success. Martial arts practice is about the development and application of power. I've learned that all success starts with personal power, whether you're a martial artist or not! ***Dynamic Components of Personal Power*** takes the transformational power of the *Black Belt* out of the *dojo* and into real life.

You can develop *Black Belt Power* to create success in your personal and professional life. You don't need to be a martial artist to make this philosophy work; you need to understand how to develop and apply power, then you need to embrace the hard work necessary to earn your *Black Belt* in the *Art of Success.*

Success is simple. It's not easy.

All you need to do to succeed in life is develop personal power by working hard and staying positive. Keep doing this over time. Then, apply your personal power to achieve anything you want. It's really that simple!

Now, why isn't it easy?

Achievement is based on action. To succeed, you must develop a positive attitude; but positive attitude alone accomplishes nothing. Many people try get-rich-quick programs that promote success solely as an exercise in mind over matter; but there's no reward without *effort.* Fewer people will roll up their sleeves and tackle the hard work necessary to develop personal power. Even fewer people will convert that power to action. Successful people do the work, despite failures and setbacks, to sustain the effort necessary to succeed.

How do I create success through personal power? Only action produces results!

The ***Dynamic Components of Personal Power*** is, above all, an action philosophy. There are plenty of systems and teachers to help you become healthy, wealthy and wise. Any system you choose will work when you apply the ideas contained in ***Dynamic Components of Personal Power.*** In fact, every effective success system utilizes these components. I've organized these principles and arranged them in diagrams to help me remember and visualize the components, and to help me put them to work in my personal and professional life. The intention of this book is to share these ideas with you.

Before we start I'm going to ask you to accept, or at least keep an open mind about, a few basic ideas that make up the core of Dynamic Components.

I'm not asking you to trust me or blindly accept what I'm saying; most of you don't even know me. Test these ideas in your own life. I can tell you that every time I meet and talk with a successful person I find that they're using most, and usually all, of the ***Dynamic Components.*** I know the components work because I constantly test them in my own personal and professional life.

I developed the ***Dynamic Components*** through my experience as a student, and later, as an instructor of martial arts. At the core, martial arts are about the development and application of power. The components we use to generate power in the *dojo (martial arts training hall)* are the same components that generate power in personal and professional life. In fact, much of the popularity of martial arts today is a result of people searching for personal development tools. The practice of martial arts is one of the most powerful tools for personal development. The mission of ***Dynamic Components*** is to translate these tools to real life.

There is plenty of everything you'll need to become powerful.

Nature supplies power in infinite quantity. All you need to do is tap into a small part of this great abundance of power to live a powerful, productive, happy and successful life.

My generation was sold a pack of lies. I'll cover the biggest of these lies in the first chapter. We were taught that it was somehow nobler to embrace poverty and weakness than to become wealthy and powerful. Popular belief held that the rich were crooks, and that only those who rejected material wealth were the ones who really served humanity. I believed most of these lies for much of my life. I was wrong and those who propagated these lies were wrong.

As I develop my personal power, I become a greater resource to those around me. I've discovered that the best thing I can do for others is to constantly improve myself.

The best way to get everything you want is to give everything you've got.

Find out exactly what it is that you have to give. Most teachers would call this your *voice*. What's yours?

Genuinely wealthy people attain wealth through giving, not taking. Please spend some time thinking about this concept; it works in material, emotional and spiritual life. Takers deplete resources quickly. Givers gain access to unlimited resources.

What do you have to offer? It can be big or small, grand or subtle; it doesn't matter. Your contribution is unique, and the surest way to change the world is to simply express yourself in your little corner. When you find whatever it is you have to give to the world that makes you feel good, you increase the power of the entire universe.

Every one of us has the capacity to develop and cultivate nearly limitless personal power.

I've been searching for success and happiness all my life. I now accept that I will continue this search for the rest of my life. I've discovered that the reason I'm alive is to find success and happiness. It took me more than thirty years to understand what I'm going to share with you in this book.

I *am* fully engaged in the never ending process of developing personal power. I *am* fully engaged in the never ending process of self perfection.

Want to take this journey with me? I can't promise you it will be easy; but if you put the ***Dynamic Components*** to work, *I can promise you will succeed!*

Top 5 Lies About Power

LIE #1: POWER CORRUPTS

Bullshit! Power does *not* have a mind. Power is *not* capable of thinking or choice. Power is simply your capacity to achieve your goals and fulfill your desires.

If your goals and desires are centered on positive values, you'll produce goodness and abundance and you'll be able to share this abundance with others.

If you're a rotten person, then you'll probably use your power to take what you want regardless of the effect on the people around you and the planet you share with them.

Whether you're a good person or a rotten person is up to you. How you use power is up to you. Without power you can't do very much. If you want to help yourself and others, you need to develop personal power. If you want to help others as well as ultimately creating happiness for yourself you'll also want to develop good character and a positive value system.

Power doesn't corrupt, it's just that corrupt people have the same access to power that you do. If you want to prevent corruption, become powerful, live a positive life and teach others to do the same.

LIE #2: POWER IS JUST FOR THE POWERFUL!

Some people *are* born with the proverbial silver spoon in their mouths. Some are born into rich families, some are also born smarter or with better health than others. True enough.

Power is not something you're born with. Power can only be developed. People born with disadvantages become powerful, and people born with every imaginable advantage can still turn out to be weak.

If you did inherit fortune, fame, good looks and intelligence, be thankful; you were blessed with some powerful resources. If you didn't, be thankful; you were given the opportunity to create your own success from scratch. You may have an advantage over those born with privilege. You may develop a true understanding and appreciation of wealth at an earlier time. You may find true wealth long before you produce material riches.

It's your nature to be powerful. It's up to you to express your nature.

LIE #3: MONEY IS POWER

In this statement you can also substitute knowledge or fame.

Money, knowledge and fame are *resources* you can access to develop and express power. They are not power in and of themselves. If they were, *all* rich and smart people would be powerful; *no* desperate or stupid people would be.

LIE #4: POWER IS CONTROL

People control power. Power without control is dangerous. In fact, you need to develop power in order to gain control. This is true of material resources, emotional resources and spiritual resources.

If you lack personal power, you cannot control these resources, these resources will control you. People become slaves to money only when they lack the power to develop control over their impulses. Greed is born in a vacuum, and the vacuum that breeds greed is an absence of personal power, discipline and compassion.

The same is true in an emotional sense. When you lack power, other people can control your emotional assets. When you're powerful, you own the resources you need to maintain control in your own life. This is particularly important when times are tough and you're emotionally vulnerable.

Don't confuse power and control. The only way to really control others is through fear and subjugation, but that kind of control invites revolt. Dictators control other people.

Inspire and motivate others. Share the power and there's little or no need for control. It's much more efficient to control conditions than to control people.

When you think you're controlling others, they may really be the ones in control. People often go along with the dictator just to make life more tolerable. Once the opportunity presents itself, most people will eventually try to free themselves from oppression. When it comes to people, control is at best a temporary illusion. Most dictators fall, and few truly win the hearts of the people.

Real control is an internal process. Learn to develop and control your own resources. Develop your own personal power. Cultivate the power in others and you'll become a leader. Leadership is your ability to bring out the best in others, and that's real power!

If you really want power in your own life and you want to have a positive impact in the lives of others, then trust is a much more powerful force than control.

LIE #5: YOU CAN'T GET IT!

A close cousin would be: "You don't deserve it."

Every human being has the capacity to develop tremendous personal power. Within the scope of your unique talents and abilities, your potential is unlimited.

I believed every one of these lies at some point in my life. I had good reason to believe these lies; they came from reliable sources. These lies came from my parents, teachers, journalists, authors, and many other people I was supposed to trust and respect. I was indoctrinated with these lies as long as I can remember. I didn't know any better. Now I do.

I'm not mad at anyone who told me these lies, and I'm not going to start this book with a negative tone. Quite the opposite: blessed with the 20/20 vision of hindsight, I can see why the people I trusted told me these lies; they cared about me!

Some people, I'm sure, propagated these lies to keep power away from me, and you. Those people think the way to preserve power is to keep it away from others. At best that's selfish, at worst it's evil.

Parents, teachers and others tell you these lies because they're trying to keep you safe! People who care about you don't want to see you take stupid chances; they don't want you to get hurt and they don't want you to end up broke and broken. They just want you to be happy- and safe.

The problem is that safe and happy don't always go together. Real reward always involves risk; to win you've got to get in the game. Discipline yourself, practice, and prepare yourself to compete. Develop the courage to face competition.

You might agree or disagree with my "Top 5 Lies About Power." That's certainly your prerogative. If you want to hold on to the idea that power corrupts, it's not for you, or you don't deserve it, I can't stop you. If you really feel that way, you may as well not waste your time reading my book.

I don't pretend to be all things to all people; I'm just sharing my own limited understanding. When something works for me, you're welcome to it. I want to be powerful. To some extent, I am powerful. I want to continue to cultivate my personal power for my benefit and the benefit of others.

I now know it is my nature to be powerful. If you believe it's your nature to be powerful, let's get started!

Go Look in the Mirror!

Student: Master, I've studied, I've worked hard, I've done all that you've asked of me. Still, I really don't understand who I am and what I'm supposed to do with my life.

Master: What do you want from me?

Student: You've lived a long time, you've been all over the world; you've done everything! Can't you tell me what to do? Can't you help me figure out who I am?

Master: I do know a teacher who can help you with this problem...I'm not him.

Student: Where can I find this teacher?

Master: Go look in the mirror!

Really!

Before we get started I want you to meet the leader of your **Personal Power Team**. I want you to meet the one person who is completely and ultimately responsible for your success.

The only person responsible for your success is the person you see in the mirror every morning.

"The person responsible for your success is the same person who brushes his teeth in your bathroom mirror!"

I believe this statement with every cell of my body. I give full credit to whoever said this; it was not me! I wish I could remember who it was; I've spent way too much time on the internet trying to find out. I'll have to be satisfied just to thank whoever coined these words; they've become an important part of my personal philosophy.

We need other people on our team. I've been blessed with wonderful teachers, advisors and mentors. I've also realized that the more I take personal responsibility for my success, the more I attract powerful people with the resources to help me further this success.

Go and look in the mirror. Smile at the person you meet there. You're going to become very close to this person as you start to explore what you need to develop power and enjoy success!

Your team starts with YOU!

All success starts with personal power. It is our nature to be happy. True happiness comes only when you feel a sense of connection with your true nature; with God, if you're religious, and other human beings. This sense of connection reveals the abundance of the universe in direct proportion to your perception of self-worth. How you value yourself is dependent on how much power you have in your life. When you feel you have power and some sense of control in your life, you'll be happier and more successful.

Weakness and poverty separate us from others and from feelings of self-worth. Nature is abundant, not impoverished. Conditions of poverty and scarcity are usually conditions created by man, and sometimes imposed on others. The imposition of scarcity and poverty on others is evil.

It is not our nature to impose evil on others. If it were, evil actions would give us feelings of connection and accomplishment. For healthy human being acts of compassion, charity, sharing, respect and loving give us the healthful feeling of connection and belonging. Acting against our compassionate and loving nature leads only to isolation. This is why some people can acquire immense material riches without experiencing true wealth and happiness. This is why people with material wealth experience joy when they share their wealth with others. Through sharing, wealth becomes even more abundant.

We are programmed for success and self-perfection. Perfection is our nature. Imperfection separates us from our true nature. Some people believe that only God can be perfect, that's fine with me; it's our imperfection that makes us perfectly human. It's our instinctive drive to better ourselves that causes us to live our lives constantly trying to connect with our natural state of happiness and to constantly strive to perfect ourselves. It's through this constant act of self-perfection we inevitably increase our connection with our true nature. I'll talk about this in detail later: *perfection is a process, not a destination.*

Self-perfection is our destiny.

Work always to improve. The most important thing you can do for others is to constantly improve yourself. When you improve yourself in body, mind and spirit you have more to share with others. To share, you must be powerful. What good do you bring the world if you share only weakness?

There's an old martial arts story about polishing a stone into a mirror. In the ancient times polishing was done by hand. Polishing a stone until it shined like a mirror required a great deal of patience, dedication and time. Eventually, with enough patience, dedication and faith we can each polish a stone into a mirror.

In this story, you are the stone! You are also the master polishing the stone. When you look into the mirror, you will really see your ***Self!***

Hard Work, Triangles and Kung Fu

I want to make two points very clear:

1. Developing personal power is hard work.

2. You can do it.

There is no shortage of self-help resources. I admit that I am myself, a self-help, self-improvement, self-motivation junky. I'm puzzled by some of the criticism of self-help and self-improvement publications. Some critics of the self-improvement genre say these materials don't work because people aren't motivated enough on their own to produce measurable results beyond these materials. Critics say that while a great speaker or writer might be able to whip you into a motivational frenzy, no system or teacher can really guarantee results once you're on your own.

I understand this criticism, given the hyped up claims made by some authors and speakers. Rather than present a dirty laundry list of such claims and my response to them, I'd rather just tell you what I believe, and more important, what you can do for yourself when you learn how to apply the ***Dynamic Components of Personal Power.***

I don't believe in guaranteed quick solutions to major problems, or instant results when facing significant challenges. I do believe any of us can get off our proverbial asses right now and start taking action toward success.

Change is hard work. Most people resist change. To make this or any other system work you've got to be willing to do the work. If you want a quick-fix solution, look somewhere else. If you want someone else to do your work for you, I'm not your guy.

In this new age of self-help, there are several teachers who preach that to find true success, all you have to do is sit and visualize and plug into the power of the universe and the work will be done for you. I disagree.

I *do believe* that you have to sit, and visualize, and plug into the power of the universe in order to make yourself more aware, and more open, to the limitless opportunity that exists all around you at all times. Then…*you've got to get to work!*

I've also found that to generate and utilize personal power, you've got to develop confidence. Power without the confidence to use it is worthless. Applying power sometimes requires great courage and spirit. Sometimes you've got to have the confidence to swim against the current. Sometimes you've got to have the courage to stand alone, particularly when doing the right thing is risky, dangerous or painful. Doing the right thing in the face of adversity requires some self-esteem.

True confidence and self-esteem are the products of hard work. We can only achieve true confidence and happiness by facing our own challenges and solving our own problems. Self-esteem is not a gift. Self-esteem is earned. Nobody can gift self-worth to another.

One of the great works of contemporary philosophy is the story of Dorothy from *The Wizard of Oz.* Dorothy had the power to go home whenever she wanted to, but first she had to face challenges, obstacles, witches, and flying monkeys before she realized this power.

Developing power is not easy. It is, however, simple.

I've found in my career as a martial artist that simple techniques are usually the most difficult to master. The mechanics of a powerful kick are relatively simple; however, it isn't easy to do the work necessary, over time, to develop a powerful kick. In our culture we're somewhat addicted to complexity. When a simple solution comes along we can be skeptical, lazy or fearful. If something is really simple, it really can't work, right?

I started my martial arts study in a system called *Kenpo.* Martial arts can often be a secretive and insular world. Some teachers forbid students from learning any other style. All martial artists hold some definite opinions about what will and will not work, but those who are more enlightened keep an open mind to new ideas and concepts and share that sense of openness with students.

I began to study with different teachers in various systems. I noticed that while there were many different paths, the destination was the same: power. Martial arts instructors like to talk about *The Way,* or what the Chinese call the *Tao.* To keep things simple, the *Tao* is the way of the universe, inclusive of as well as above and beyond our capacity for understanding; more on that later. Each instructor preached about the truth of *The Way,* yet strangely, many were critical of a different perspective or path.

I'm not exactly sure exactly when or how this happened, but at some point I began to realize that while differences made each style interesting, the real power lies in what makes these systems similar rather than different. I started to wonder which principles, consistent in each system, give us access to power.

Once I began to identify these elemental principles of power, I realized that ***everyone can access these principles.***

The Chinese words "Kung Fu" literally mean a high level of achievement through great effort. We'll examine this concept in great detail in another chapter. For now, it's enough to understand that *Kung Fu* is not necessarily the name of a particular martial arts style, but rather a level of achievement you can realize in any art, including business and professional arts.

Every human endeavor can be considered an art. Art is how we express ourselves creatively. We're all familiar with the most obvious artistic pursuits like painting, photography, acting, writing and music; however, we can express our human potential through any human endeavor from collecting garbage to writing music. The point is that if we approach any task with an understanding of *Kung Fu,* we approach each task as an artist.

In my life so far, I've used many avenues to express my creativity. I enjoy writing, music and photography. Most of my adult life I've been a martial artist.

As I continually became more confident in my abilities and my understanding of martial arts, I began to recognize specific key *dynamic components* that helped me enjoy and improve my artistic expression. As a martial artist, the ultimate manifestation of my creative expression was the execution of technique...with POWER!

As my understanding increased, I began to realize that these key *dynamic components* were the essential ingredients needed to cultivate and increase power.

I started to analyze each movement in my practice through the basic elements that gave that movement power. I started to understand that these same principles could work in other areas of my life as well as in my martial arts. As I learned to develop power for martial arts, I began to apply this understanding to develop power in these other areas including business, personal relations, even in my spiritual exploration.

I also realized that whenever I ignored or tried to work outside these principles, life got a lot tougher! I started to pay attention to successful and happy people. I started to pay attention to what I was doing when I felt successful, happy and fulfilled.

I also started to pay attention when people were miserable. I started to pay attention to what I was missing at times when I felt worthless and needy, or at times when success seemed a little beyond my reach.

Then, I discovered the power of Triangles!

I have a fascination with science and physics, but I'm only blessed with a layman's capacity for understanding these subjects. To help me better understand these principles, I began to study more about physics and power from a scientific perspective. I immediately realized a connection between physics and the essence of martial arts training.

For example, when developing a strong stance, angles are very important. The strongest stances always contain some form of the triangle, three lines supporting one another. The triangle is the strongest shape in engineering. Each side supports the other; diminish one side or close one angle and the integrity of the structure is compromised.

At this time I was becoming more intrigued with the philosophical concepts of Asian martial arts. I studied these philosophies to deepen my own understanding, and to share these ideas with my students. I wanted to try to simplify these complex philosophical ideas into a form I could understand and apply in my life, and to teach these practical concepts in language that would resonate with the American ear.

Again and again I found I needed three words or concepts to translate the true meaning of any single Asian philosophical concept. No more, no less! To be honest, it just worked out that way, again and again!

Let's use *Kung Fu* as an example. As I said earlier, the literal translation would be achievement through great effort. That's not quite the whole story.

There are many heroic stories of success in battle and in life from the martial arts traditions of Asia. The heroes in these great stories always seemed to possess incredible ***motivation*** and ***discipline.*** I found these to be key elements in developing power which could produce victory and success. However, to really translate the essence of the words "Kung Fu," we've got to understand and appreciate one more powerful component…

The third component is ***time.*** In most stories the hero only realizes his true potential and reward after working hard and facing challenges, *for a long time!* It may take only a short time to develop competency and even expertise in some areas, but only over time do we realize ***mastery.*** The essential quality of *The Master* is **wisdom,** developed through *experience,* over *time.*

So, to fully express the meaning of *Kung Fu* I needed three English words:

- ✍ **Motivation**
- ✍ **Discipline**
- ✍ **Time**

I chose these words to be the components of the *Kung Fu Triangle,* and the root of the ***Dynamic Components of Personal Power*** philosophy.

Just as the triangle provides the most stable shape for physical design, the triangle also provides the best diagram to represent my philosophical understanding of power and the concepts that support the development and application of power. Each side is mutually supportive. Diminish one side and power is reduced.

Dynamic Components of Personal Power is based on three basic *Triangles.* Each triangle diagrams three components necessary to understand, develop, cultivate and apply personal power.

Three is simple, and it's easy to remember 3 bits of information at a time. In fact, current research shows that our memory deals best with information in groups, or "chunks," of 4 bits, plus or minus a couple! Three components make an easy grouping to remember. We'll stick with this formula!

You could make a decent argument that life is complex. It's complicated to develop and apply the skills we need to face everyday challenges, much less prepare for future opportunities.

One of the great insights I found in Eastern philosophy and science was the process of looking at a complex idea as a whole. No matter how many people live on this planet, we're all simply human. We're parts of a bigger whole. Our life works like this. We may not be able to identify every part of our body; most of us can't name any more than a handful of our 108 separate bones. Taken as a whole, however, our body works quite nicely; most of the time without any conscious effort on our part.

Most people in Western culture consider a car a simple and necessary part of daily life. Few truly understand how a car really works. To most of us, a car works through the application of two basic operations; turn the key, and step on the gas pedal. Occasionally we have to get out of the car and add fuel! Simple!

If, however, you're an engineer looking at design drawings for a new model, the car is a complex integration of mechanical and energetic form and function.

Which is the true car? The complex set of tangible mechanical parts operating in perfect synchronicity, or the simple energetic process of jumping in and deciding where to go?

Actually, both! From either perspective we're still talking about a car.

Now, imagine a Western scientist and an Eastern scientist transported into our century from 600 years ago. Imagine both of them discovering at a car for the first time.

To understand the car, the Western scientist might take the car apart and look at the complex interaction of all the parts. This *mechanical* perspective is certainly a valid way to look at things. This is the kind of thinking that DaVinci utilized to understand flight, hundreds of years before someone applied his ideas and produced the airplane. He was a master of dissection and understood complex processes through intricate mechanical interactions.

The Eastern scientist might watch the car and describe its movement from an *energetic* perspective. The Eastern philosopher or scientist might describe the car as an object that seems to propel itself after taking on an essential energy, or "Chi," contained in an amber liquid. This liquid needs to be replenished to provide the energy needed to move the car. This energy is then released, subject to the commands of the human driver, manifest in the forward movement of the car. The driver decides where the car will go and how fast it will get there, and so the mind of the driver becomes an essential part in the operation of this thing called a car.

Both perspectives reveal part of the truth. Today's great thinkers often combine knowledge of both energetic and mechanical systems to seek a deeper understanding of nature's operation. We live in an age when borders between philosophical and scientific perspectives are merging. Einstein transcended the gap between what was evident and what was possible and gave birth to the most dynamic period in scientific history. Quantum physics validates the ancient masters' perspective that energy and matter are not separate entities, but rather different qualities of the same phenomenon we attempt to describe as reality.

I'm no Einstein or DaVinci, however, I do appreciate the power in the creative processes they utilized to arrive at their ideas. The more I explore my own talents and abilities the more I recognize a consistent theme that flows through me, and you, as well as Einstein and DaVanci, and all the other great thinkers through the ages. We all have access to human power through the same basic processes; *we're all human.*

To facilitate my own understanding, I distilled the complex idea of personal power to these simple and practical components. As I started to appreciate these basic processes, I labeled them the ***Dynamic Components of Personal Power.***

Later we'll explore specific definitions of power as it applies to mechanical processes in physics; the definition of power as it relates to human behavior is subject to various interpretations.

The psychological or philosophical definition of power is usually related to its application. In using the word power to describe human behavior you need to consider feeling. Feeling is the communication between mind and body, and is completely dependent on your perspective. Your perspective is the product of your unique experiences and frame of reference.

There are few topics more complicated than the workings of the human mind, so developing, understanding and applying power can be looked at as a complex process.

I believe that many people avoid developing personal power simply because just seems too complicated or difficult.

The *Triangles* are simple diagrams I'll use to simplify this process. All I've really done is to reduce the development and application of power to bite size chunks.

Quick review:

I use the triangle for three reasons. First, every time I've tried to simplify these concepts in my experience, I end up with three fundamental principles. Second, the triangle is the most stable shape in construction. Third, we tend to remember sets of three items easily. To be honest, I personally wanted a system that's easy to remember!

Developing power is simple; it's also hard work. Everyone has the capacity to do this work. In fact, the work of developing power becomes, in itself, part of your expression of personal power.

As you begin this work you'll develop a personal vision of success and choose supportive goals and objectives to support your vision. You'll realize that within the scope of your talents and abilities, everything you want to accomplish can be done. You'll also realize a new capacity for expanding your talents and abilities.

The work of expanding your potential is done by inches, but as the iconic coach Vince Lombardi once said, "Inches make a champion." [1]

"Start by doing what's necessary, then what's possible, and then suddenly you are doing the impossible." [2]

Saint Francis of Assisi

Your goals and objectives are sometimes daunting and may even, at times, seem impossible. However, every great accomplishment is simply a series of smaller steps.

"The journey of a thousand miles must begin with the first step."

Power: A Definition!

I can share the "secret" of power with you in just a few seconds...

Power is expressed effectively when you apply three basic components: ***Balance, Focus*** and ***Timing.*** You develop power through ***Motivation,*** and ***Discipline,*** over ***Time.*** The sources of human power are found in the ***Body, Mind*** and ***Spirit.*** In order to cultivate power you need to constantly develop and nurture your body, your mind and your spirit.

That's it! These are the Dynamic Components of Personal Power.

You can spend the rest of your life working on, with, and through these basic components to develop and cultivate power and achieve your personal vision of success. For now, just keep these basic principles in mind as we define exactly what power is, and why developing power is so important to a happy and productive life.

The primary dictionary definition of *power* is:

"The ability or capacity to perform or act effectively."[3]

Developing personal power is really the process of developing the *"ability to act effectively."* If you want to accomplish your goals and live life the way you choose, you've got to start by developing your capacity to act effectively to achieve those goals; you've got to start by developing your personal power.

Many people say knowledge is power. Others say money is power; I disagree. Knowledge is not in itself power; neither is money, fame or favors. Knowledge, money, and I'll add fame and goodwill, are not in themselves *abilities.* These are *reservoirs* in which you'll gather and store *potential* for power.

In ***Think and Grow Rich*** Napoleon Hill, one of the great pioneers of the self-improvement age says:

"Power may be defined as 'organized and intelligently directed knowledge.'"[4]

In physics:

"Power is defined as the work done per unit of time or as the rate at which work is done"[5]

Power implies action. Power means you're doing something. How much power you express depends on how much you're doing and how long it takes you to do it.

As I said, knowledge, money and goodwill are *reservoirs* in which we can store *potential power*. The action of gathering knowledge, money and goodwill requires power; we need to work to increase these reserves.

Through action we transform our reserves of potential power into applicable power. I live near the Androscoggin River in Maine. Near my home is a large power dam. Behind the dam the water is very deep and usually looks very calm. This water is like knowledge, money and goodwill. The water contains enormous potential; however, power is only measured when the water flows through the turbines of the power generator. The generator transforms the potential energy contained in the water into the electrical power we use to make our lives productive and comfortable.

To start this process, to initiate action to accumulate resources and put your resources to work, you need a spark. This spark is an idea. Everything you accomplish, great and small, starts with an idea. Every great accomplishment from rubbing two sticks together to make fire to man's first trip to the moon started with an idea.

Each of us has the capacity to generate this initial spark. It's up to you to fan that spark into a flame to attain your own personal goals and create your success.

The cycle always starts with you. Only you can develop your personal power and do the work necessary to acquire knowledge, money, fame, and goodwill. Accumulating knowledge requires learning; acquiring money usually requires work. Fame involves introducing yourself to others and goodwill is the result of your efforts in relationships with others including favors, kindness, leadership, and caring.

Once acquired, knowledge, money, fame and goodwill can then be stored just as batteries store electricity. The capacity of a battery is measured in *volts:* units of *potential energy.* Knowledge, money, fame and goodwill are stored as your personal power *voltage.* The greater store of personal power voltage you have, the more work you can do. That work in turn produces more energy, some of which you can use to recharge your stores of knowledge, money, fame and goodwill. This cycle is regenerating the same way your car first draws on its battery to start the engine, then recharges the battery as you run down the road.

Let's take another look at the definition of power as it relates to physics. In physics power is defined as "The rate at which work is done, expressed as the amount of work per unit time and commonly measured in units such as the watt and horsepower."[6]

As I share my observations and ideas with you, this point is going to become very important, *personal power* is what we're getting done, over time. In other words, we're going to discuss personal power in terms of our capacity to accomplish our goals, but we're also going to measure our personal power in terms of what we're actually accomplishing along the way. You can work hard for a short time and produce a lot of results, or power. You can also work a little bit each day over time and accomplish great things. You can work hard and waste energy, or you can use energy efficiently and produce more power with less work.

Develop efficiency and your work will produce greater results. You don't want to waste your energy or your time; when you properly utilize your energy and time, you'll operate at peak efficiency and you'll develop the capacity to generate tremendous power. As you make your personal power machine more efficient, you lighten the load and produce the best possible results in proportion to your efforts.

I teach my martial arts students: ***"never confuse exertion with power."*** Make this mistake and you'll work awfully hard yet produce very little. When an engine is not working efficiently due to lack of care or tuning, it can use a lot of fuel in exchange for very little power. In human terms, when you're not operating efficiently, you experience stress. Eventually, something breaks.

The key to efficiency lies in the second principle in the *Power Triangle:* ***Focus.*** You first need to develop rooting or *balance,* in other words create a sound foundation. With a sound foundation you're better able to apply power with *focus* or concentrated effort at the appropriate time. That's power!

The key to the *application* of personal power is to develop your ability or capacity to access and apply balance, focus and timing.

Is Power Good or Evil?

Let's take a moment and head off what can often become an emotionally charged, wasteful and self-defeating argument.

Is power *good* or is it *evil?* If you want to apply the ideas I'm going to share with you it's important that we agree on this point. Power in and of itself is neither good nor evil. These qualities only become important in the *application* of power.

Is electricity good or evil? Electricity feels pretty good when you're using it to heat your home on a cold winter day. If you accidentally stick your finger into a live socket, I suppose you might consider it evil. In both cases, it's not the electricity itself but your perspective that defines the application as good or evil. Good and evil are definitions we assign; not inherent qualities of electricity itself.

In the same way, power can be applied toward good or evil ends. Even a rudimentary study of history will give you plenty of examples of each. What's important to our discussion is that I'm going to assume *(and hope)* that you'll cultivate personal power to improve your life and the lives of those around you. Since I have no control over how you'll apply your personal power, this is the best that I can do.

The problem is that rotten people have access to the same power that we do. I'm a realist; I know that some people will develop power and use it to evil ends. That's been going on a long, long time and there's not much I can do about it. What I can do is develop my personal power and use my power ethically for my benefit and the benefit of others.

The fundamental problem is not that some people will develop power for evil purposes; despite my best efforts, they will. What I worry about most is that too many people are unwilling to do the work needed to develop personal power for self-improvement and the benefit of others!

There is a terrible waste going on in our culture. We're squandering our most precious resource: Too many people waste their true human potential. Rather than focusing on what other people may be doing or not doing; it's a lot more powerful to focus on what each of us can accomplish! It's much more productive to take action than to waste time complaining.

"It's better to light a candle than to curse the darkness."[7]

Chinese proverb

The less power you have, the fewer choices you have. When you don't develop your personal power, you surrender your fundamental freedom. When you don't have the power to choose, you become dependent on others.

With all our prosperity and abundance there are many who don't seem to realize their potential; this is a great tragedy of our culture and times. In a land of opportunity too many people choose not to see the possibilities.

I'm not denying that there are people who legitimately lack some of the resources to become successful. However that's not really the problem for most of us. Some of you may have been born into money; many of us have faced some degree of poverty. We cannot control where we are born or what family or society we're born into. Above all, none of us can control the conditions of nature!

It's also true that despite sincere and dedicated efforts, any of us can be reduced to desperate conditions through circumstances beyond our control. Still, the vast majority of us have access to nearly unlimited opportunity and potential and everyone, regardless of current conditions, possesses at least some capacity to initiate change. The examples of people who have risen above poverty, disease and ignorance to change the world would fill a library. In fact, most of our libraries *are* filled with these stories!

The larger problem is that most people are either ignorant of their potential or worse; don't want to expend the effort necessary to cultivate personal power.

I am terrified that so many of us will simply never develop and share our own personal power! At the core of my personal belief system is the faith that *most* people who realize their true potential will use it in a positive manner. I want to help more people realize this potential and develop this power. I know that most people who hear this message have the capacity to design their own vision of success and go for it.

Develop personal power, reach our fullest human potential and share that with others. That's how we can each change the world for the better.

The Selflessness of Self Improvement

"The most important thing I can do for others is to constantly improve myself."

This has become my personal mantra. I've focused much of my time and effort over the past several years studying success. I've found incredible parallels between martial artists who are successful in the *dojo, (martial arts training hall),* and successful people in the real world. Most of all, I've found that the people who do the greatest good for others are those who dedicate themselves to constant personal development and self-improvement.

So how do you define success? Your view of personal success may be a lot different than mine. Do you want to make a lot of money? Would you like to have the resources to spend more time volunteering or doing charity work? Maybe right now your vision of success means completing school or getting a promotion or landing a good job to better support your family. For many of you I'm sure success means raising happy and successful children.

Take a few moments and relax. Put this book down and just spend a few minutes thinking about how you define your own personal success, today. Think about what your life will likely be in ten or so years. If your life continues on its present course, will you see yourself as successful in ten years?

Now, let's get back to work. Put aside any personal definition of success and define it in terms of simple principles. A simple dictionary definition of success is: *"the favorable or prosperous termination of attempts or endeavors."*[8] Boring!

First of all, part of my personal vision of success is to keep on keeping on! I don't want to retire in the traditional sense. I want to have meaningful work to do until I die.

How about the following definition?

"Success is the outcome, determined by your ability to recognize and exploit opportunity, at any given moment."

In order to recognize opportunity you've got to have the potential power contained in knowledge. To exploit this opportunity you've got to have the potential power of talent, skill and resources. Simply put, you've got to have some personal power in order to recognize and take advantage of opportunity.

The good news is that opportunity is an inexhaustible resource. For those of us fortunate enough to live in America or other developed democratic countries, opportunities are limited only by talent, ability, desire, ambition, and *personal choice!*

Nearly every month I meet someone who tells me he can't realize his dreams because of circumstances beyond his control. These circumstances usually include lack of education, responsibilities of family or lack of financial resources. All these circumstances are *can be* the result of personal choices. Of course, the earlier you learn to identify goals and develop your vision of personal success the better prepared you'll be to make choices that produce the results you desire. I can state from personal experience that it's never too late to start this process; I've made poor choices and I've learned to make better ones.

The point is that to attain success you've got to begin to cultivate your greatest resource: your own personal power! Let's look at some areas of life where your power will be cultivated. In other words, where's the power now?

Take a few minutes and consider the following list. Which of these items would you consider a *power resource* in your life? Are there some areas I've left out or others you might consider valuable?

- **Knowledge**
- **Health/Fitness**
- **Spirituality or Personal Faith**
- **Goodwill & Fame (Connections to Others)**
- **Money & Material Possessions**

Your list may differ from mine. I tend to simplify ideas to their most basic components. For me these areas make up my *Personal Power Batteries.* Every productive endeavor in my life relating to my development of personal power feeds into one of these categories. When the timing is right to apply power I draw on these personal power reserves to transform potential into action. I constantly apply the ***Dynamic Components*** to recharge or build-up my *Personal Power Batteries.* The greater charge of energy in my batteries, the more power I can access when opportunity appears.

Trying to exploit an opportunity without a stored charge of personal power is like trying to find your way in a storm when the batteries in your flashlight are dead. There might be an opportunity at right in front of you, but you won't see it in the dark.

Skills are the tools you use to exploit opportunities. I make two guarantees to my students that are working toward black belt. First, the knowledge and self-awareness developed in earning a black belt will give them the tools to do anything they want in life, within the scope of their talents and abilities. Second, they'll learn how to recognize and develop these talents and abilities.

I'm a realist. It's naïve to simply tell someone "you can do anything you want in life." The fact is that everyone has natural abilities and talents…and limitations. Talents are shaped by particular interests, sometimes instinctive, most often nurtured by the environment in which you're raised.

However, there are always opportunities to discover and cultivate new, innate and inherited talents and abilities.

There are countless cases of those who explode beyond conventional limitations. How could a man 5 foot 7 inches tall succeed in professional basketball? Spud Webb was that man! He played NBA basketball for 12 successful seasons. In 1986 he won the *Slam Dunk* competition against men 7 feet tall.

Many people believe the popular myth that a martial artist can defeat any opponent, even one many times his or her size. The fact is, however, that in real combat a larger or stronger opponent has distinct advantage, all other things being equal. The key to victory is to identify and exploit your opponent's weaknesses and, more important, to understand and develop your own strengths and use them to your advantage.

First, develop an awareness of your own natural talents and abilities. Then, choose which talents and abilities you want to cultivate.

What's your passion? One of the most predominant qualities of success is that successful people tend to be aware of their natural talents or calling. Successful people tend to spend choose work that satisfies their personal interests and passions. They choose work that's in synch with their talents and abilities, or they work to increase talent and ability in response to their passion and interests.

Once you identify your talents, abilities and passion, you can work toward *mastery. Mastery* is the development of a skill to the level where others consider your skills to be worthy of respect. In today's martial arts world, anyone can claim the title of *Master* and many attain the title by passing a series of tests. In ancient times a teacher was called *Master* by those who respected and valued his teaching.

In 2006 an extensive study was done to find the secret ingredient to personal mastery. Scientists studied people who had mastered several disciplines, particularly chess. The data showed that the most important element in mastering any skill is: ***dedicated and focused practice over an extended period of time.*** Martial artists have known this for hundreds, if not thousands of years!

Remember our introduction to the concept of *Kung Fu? Kung Fu* refers to an achievement produced by *dedicated effort over time.* This concept is so important to the development of personal power that I diagramed *Kung Fu* in one of our 3 major *Triangles.* The components of *Kung Fu* are ***motivation, discipline*** and ***time.***

Concentrated effort, *over time,* is an essential ingredient in self-improvement and personal development. In martial arts, we often express this kind of directed effort as *mindfulness.* Mindful effort is always more efficient, more effective and more productive. Develop mindfulness and you become more aware of your place in nature and in the lives of those around you. Through this process, your personal quest to develop power becomes a positive force in the lives of others.

I sincerely hope your intention is to benefit those around you and the world in general. I believe the beginning of all charity starts by improving the *Self* and accessing personal power. As you increase personal power, you become a greater resource for others and for the world at large.

Keys to Mindful Self-Improvement

There are some simple keys to the practice of mindful self-improvement. These keys unlock the principles that lead to personal power:

- ✍ **Dedicated Introspection.**
- ✍ **The ability to accept criticism.**
- ✍ **Embracing *perfection* as a process.**

Dedicated introspection is the process of constantly looking in the mirror first when analyzing thoughts and actions. Make looking in the mirror a habit, a discipline. Constantly review the results or consequences of your thoughts and actions. This reflection must be based on your core values, principles and ethics.

Accept responsibility for your thoughts and actions and your thoughts and actions will generate meaningful experiences that move consistently toward self-improvement, abundance and later, generosity. Personal responsibility is defined by your acknowledgement that every thought and action affects the world and people around you. The development of power devoid of personal responsibility is a tragic waste of human energy and leads to abuse.

The practice of dedicated introspection requires the acceptance of personal responsibility. It requires that you embrace accountability before assigning blame. A particular failure may not be your fault, however; *you are always responsible for your response to failure.*

Sometimes luck and circumstances beyond your control do play a part in both success and failure. Still, introspection is always useful, and reveals guidance to direct your next action.

Every disaster is an opportunity! However, you can only see the opportunity in disaster when you learned to take a good look at yourself and trained yourself to respond according to your own unique awareness and perspective using your own unique talents and abilities.

The ability to accept criticism is the next key to self-improvement. Criticism is a reflection from another person's point of view. If dedicated introspection is the action of looking at yourself in the mirror, criticism is what you see when someone else holds the mirror!

Sensei is the title given to a teacher in Japanese martial arts. The best working definition of *Sensei* is: *"one who went before";* obviously an appropriate title for a teacher.

This title recognizes that a teacher is someone who has already traveled the route you're seeking, or at least part of it. In traditional Japanese martial training there is very little questioning of the teacher. The student is expected to follow instructions and accept criticism gratefully. There is obviously a great deal of trust implied in this relationship. A teacher is very carefully chosen by a student, and students are carefully qualified by a teacher.

Constructive criticism is becoming a lost art in modern culture. Self-centered behavior diminishes the benefits of productive criticism. Today, criticism is often seen as an insult, a put-down, a way to keep us in our place. Of course, many self-styled critics in our culture have lost the art of *constructive* criticism. The critic has become an icon and criticism a marketable pop-culture commodity. The art of criticism as a tool for teaching is lost when the critic becomes, or considers himself, more important than the subject.

A sincere martial artist constantly seeks constructive criticism. When a teacher can no longer identify areas for improvement, it's time to find another teacher. Your next teacher has to have greater insight, or a different perspective or skill. A sincere martial artist considers criticism an expression of respect.

I often tell my students that if I'm criticizing, I care. They only need to worry when I start to ignore them!

It's also important to learn how to be self-critical. Learning to accept the criticism of others gives you access to experience, wisdom and consideration beyond your current capacity and insight. Self-criticism is a powerful tool for development. As you develop the skill of constructive self-criticism, you train yourself to be your own teacher.

Caring critics can become your most valuable teachers. Learn to choose your teachers carefully and to recognize them when they arrive unannounced in your life! Today you have almost unlimited access to great teachers through books, the internet and other media. The world's greatest teachers are available to you whether you meet them face to face, through books, video or on-line. Still, there's no substitute for direct contact and a personal relationship with your closest teachers. Your *personal teachers* are those who show a particular sincere interest in the details of your quest, and are usually those vested somehow in your success.

Perfection is a process, not a destination.

The idea of perfection as a final goal or physical state of being is crippling to any self-improvement effort.

Have you ever heard the story of the donkey and the carrot? In this story, when the donkey refuses to pull the cart, you just strap a carrot to stick and hang it in front of his face; he'll keep chasing after the carrot and end up pulling the cart. At first this sounds like a clever idea except for one vital point: *you're a person, not a donkey!*

When you think of perfection as an end or a destination you become just like the donkey chasing the carrot. The problem is that in chasing the carrot, the donkey is never aware of the journey. He doesn't see what's going on around him and since he's a donkey, he probably doesn't care.

Unlike the donkey, you'll eventually figure out that you're never getting any closer to the carrot! As a human being blessed with self-awareness, you'll inevitably get tired of chasing the carrot. To be successful, you've got to buy into the idea that the reward is not the carrot; the reward is everything you do and everyplace you go while you're chasing your carrot.

Success is intertwined with failure. The greatest failure is not enjoying or reaping the benefits of each journey. When you embrace perfection as a *process*, you can enjoy the trip. Maintain focus, keep an eye on the prize, but make sure you're also looking around as you travel. Get the lay of the land and pay attention to the steps that get you closer, the steps that cause you to stumble or slip, and the steps that don't go anywhere at all. Every single step is an important part of your journey.

When you embrace perfection as a process, you're moving toward success and perfection whether or not you ever reach the carrot. The truth is that in most cases, the carrot is pretty stale at the end of the trip anyway. You don't want to miss a fresh, delicious and nutritious salad along the way!

You could probably come up with enough information to support the argument that nobody is perfect. Many people feel that since there's no way to achieve absolute perfection, it just isn't worth trying. This self-defeating argument prowls well below the ideal of perfection and causes you to compare yourself with others. The danger here is that you might ignore or pass on an opportunity just because you're never going to be *perfect.*

Forgetaboutit!

If you have an opportunity that feels right, go for it! Don't worry about being perfect; enjoy the process of perfection. I guarantee you'll enjoy some remarkable rewards when you embrace the process of self-perfection.

Have you ever wanted to learn a musical instrument? Have you ever decided not to bother just because you didn't think you'd be any good at it?

By the way, there is strong scientific evidence to support the theory that learning to play music significantly improves brain power. There is also great evidence that says playing an instrument improves health by through relaxation and stimulation of the "immune response."

Learning and enjoying an instrument produces benefits even if you never play in public for anyone. You don't need to compare your musical abilities to anyone else's. If music isn't for you, find another art or craft. Any creative process will serve the same needs. "Don't dream it, be it!"

When you embrace perfection as a process *there is no place you're going to.* As you participate in the process you're already there! This way of looking at things in no way devalues goals and accomplishments. Every goal in life is related to every activity in which you participate. Learning how to play a guitar just might be the key ingredient in your development as a captain of industry, a doctor or a world leader. Einstein believed that playing the violin connected him with the harmony of the universe! Music provided his spiritual connection to the feeling that the universe operated with a powerful and subtle order.

Einstein's love of music played a huge part in his scientific and philosophical thinking; and he changed the way we look at the world forever.

One of the reasons I continue my martial arts practice is that this practice benefits and influences every other activity in my life. In my experience, I've found the practice of martial arts to be one of the most powerful activities available to develop personal power and success.

As I continue my process of self-improvement I'm actively participating in the process of perfection. In this way I am empowered rather than discouraged when I face a challenge or experience frustration.

"Frustration is the well from which all wisdom springs!"

You can choose to constantly remind yourself that you're not perfect, or you can choose to experience the process of perfection in every moment.

The Dynamic Components of Personal Power

Now we get to work!

There's a tense scene in the movie *Apollo 13* in which the engineers at Houston Control are trying to figure out how much time the astronauts have left before all hope is lost. The focus up to then had been on the oxygen supply aboard the space craft. One of the flight engineers interrupts the meeting and insists that oxygen isn't the main concern; the real trouble is that the spacecraft's batteries don't have enough electrical power to get the astronauts back to earth. He makes his argument: "Power is *everything.* Without it they don't talk to us, they don't correct their trajectory, they don't turn the heat shield around," you get the point…

"It's all about power!"

It's all about power here on earth as well. Human beings need power. We need power to operate the mind and the body. It all starts with power, and when our power runs out human life as we know it ceases to exist.

It's not only your nature to be powerful; there's nothing more essential to life than power! You started this journey to develop *personal* power. You're going to use this power to create the life you want for yourself.

Through my martial arts practice I've realized that the same principles that help me generate power in a punch or kick are the same principles that help me develop power in real life. Don't worry; ***you don't need to become a martial artist to utilize these principles.*** Everyone can apply the ***Dynamic Components*** to create success in personal and professional life.

I'm often asked how and why I got started in martial arts. The truth is that I originally started training in martial arts because I had no sense of my own personal power. I possessed very little self-worth and I really did not think anything I was doing was of much value to anyone else. I was directed to martial arts by some caring mentors who saw that I might develop some self-esteem, and realize some of my true potential, through martial arts practice. They were right, and I'm very thankful that my heart was open enough at the time to accept their guidance.

The more I learned about myself I realized that like the people I admired, I too could accomplish some remarkable things. Each new accomplishment became a step on the path to future successes. I learned to transmute feelings of failure into learning. I stopped using failure as a personal retreat and started to open myself to possibility and opportunity. Through my training I realized that the personal power I was developing in martial arts was beginning to carry over to life at work, relationships and the rest of my life.

Generating power is simple; it is not easy.

I don't consider myself any sort of genius, and I can't tell you I came to these realizations easily or instantly; it took a great deal of time and a great deal of work and my work is not over. My hope is that sharing my ideas with you will help you access personal power more directly than I did. Selfishly, the process of teaching ***Dynamic Components*** also helps *me* as I constantly re-examine and refine this philosophy for more effective and efficient application.

No matter what anyone shares with you, you still have to do the work for yourself. You need to take the time necessary to cultivate a positive attitude and an understanding of personal power. What better way to spend your time? I say this again and again, but there's nothing more important you can do for yourself and for others than to constantly improve your *Self.*

So, what exactly are the Dynamic Components of Personal Power and how do you apply them?

The ***Dynamic Components of Personal Power*** are nine basic principles I've isolated to help me understand where power comes from, how to cultivate power, and how to apply power to produce results. I've organized the *Components* into 3 groups and produced three *Triangles* to diagram these ideas in a form we can all use as a simple graphical reference. I use the triangle because it's the strongest shape in engineering and I felt I wanted a picture that would reinforce the strength of the *Components* in building personal power. By using a triangle you'll see the components as mutually reinforcing; each side supports and reinforces the integrity of the whole design.

I kept trying to simplify these concepts to their most basic elements, and I kept coming down to three components in each area. As it turns out, this works pretty well since the human brain seems to remember groups of three easily and to be honest, it just kept working out that way!

We're going to start at the end, and end up at the beginning. I'll start with how you're going to use power, we'll then talk about how to cultivate power, and finally we'll explore the sources of human power.

The first triangle is the ***Power Triangle.*** The *Power Triangle* represents how we use or apply power; how power is manifest. The *Power Triangle* contains the components necessary to produce results!

Power is manifest through 3 ***Dynamic Components:***

- **Balance**
- **Focus**
- **Timing**

Pay attention to all three components and power flows efficiently and effectively to produce results. Ignore one of these components and power is diminished, as well as your desired results.

As I said, I'm starting at the end. Ultimately, the goal is to utilize personal power to achieve your personal vision of success. Having some idea of where you're going greatly improves your chances of getting there!

One of the great teachers of our time, Dr. Stephen Covey, identified *The 7 Habits of Highly Effective People.* One of Dr. Covey's most important principles is to "Begin with the

End in Mind." Successful people tend to think about the *big picture* first, and then worry about the details. Brilliant achievers often make up their minds to do something without any idea about how they're going to do it; the how part flows from a commitment to their goal or idea.

The first step toward any achievement is to create a goal. A goal will sharpen your focus; from there you can develop a task list full of items targeted specifically to the achievement of your goal.

Unfortunately, many people start with the details, then develop a list of tasks, and *hope* that all this work will lead somewhere. I'm talking about having a clear direction in your life so you have the power to choose your destiny. Be the leader of your own life; be the one to choose where you're going and how you're going to get there. With this mindset you're setting the pace rather than trying to keep pace with others.

In business, I use a process I call *Revenue Based Planning.* At weekly meetings in each of my organizations we start with our "end in mind," particularly how much revenue we intend to generate. For each business, we've reduced our main streams of revenue production to triangles, *of course!* After identifying 3 broad revenue areas, we start to brainstorm and develop tasks that will produce results in each area. Within each area we address whether we're in balance as an organization based on our values, principles and code of ethics. Next, we decide how best to focus our efforts and determine the most effective timing.

In business, revenue is the direct measurement of how effectively you generate and apply power. You can apply the same *Components* to develop business power that you're going to use to develop personal power.

To translate these ideas to personal power, just change the name to *Personal Success Based Planning.* What do you want to do? What do you *really* want to do? When do want to achieve your goals? Don't worry about how you're going to do it yet, you've got time to worry about that later.

You may be rolling your eyes now; another book that says "set goals" and the world will be at your feet; *not exactly.*

Some of you might be saying, "I set goals all the time!" Some of you probably do set goals, and regularly achieve them; if so, excellent!

Others might have a case of "Fred Flintstone Syndrome." If your memory extends back a little farther it might be "Ralph Kramden Syndrome." Both these conditions describe someone who constantly has a big idea, but keeps getting kicked in the proverbial ass; *"If it weren't for bad luck, I'd have no luck at all."*

First of all, goal setting really is this important. Master Jhoon Rhee built one of the most successful martial arts organizations in the world. I had the incredible opportunity to hear him speak as he addressed a group of martial art professionals. His mission was to convince us to become successful, and to share our success for the benefit of our communities.

Master Rhee teaches that ***"the source of all human energy is a goal."*** Nature provides us with limitless human energy; however, to convert that energy to action we need a goal.

When you start with the goal then task from there, you become much more discriminating about which tasks will be the most productive. Without a clearly defined goal you can spend a great deal of time and energy putting out fires and chasing your tail. Without a strong commitment to a goal it becomes very easy to generate *busy work* that may or may not produce any significant results.

Have you ever drafted a list that ends up full of tasks, only to find your list doesn't do a damn thing to move you any closer to your own goals? How many times have you spent a day running all over the place doing family errands without taking any time for yourself? How many times have you analyzed all this busy work only to realize that most of what you did really wasn't appreciated or ultimately wasn't productive?

This condition can happen when your priorities are out of synch with the priorities of other people in your life. This happens even within a family. A family is an organization; the family organization would operate much more effectively and efficiently with a clear set of over-arching goals that support the group, and each individual family member.

The most important thing we can do for others is to constantly improve ourselves.

Make sure to schedule time for constant self-improvement in each key area of life. Most people would place health and financial security in key positions. You've got to dedicate time to activities that will help you progress and maintain abundance in each of these areas. Setting goals will help you keep your eye on the prize and help you avoid inefficient and costly distractions.

In a healthy and happy relationship, the goals of the group and the individuals in the group are mutually supportive. This principle works for a couple, a family or a corporation.

Personal power is expressed through the components of *balance, focus* and *timing*…once you identify a particular goal. Working toward your goals with balance, focus and timing dramatically increases your chances for success.

The *Power Triangle* is supported by two other triangles. Working back, the next triangle contains the components for power development. This is the ***Kung Fu Triangle.*** Earlier I said that *Kung Fu* literally means an achievement through great effort; the literal translation just doesn't do full justice to the concept.

There's no one word in English that directly translates as *Kung Fu.* Any discussion of achievement and effort has to include motivation and discipline. As we learned earlier, the final ingredient that completes the full meaning of *Kung Fu* is *time.* Lot's of things can be achieved in little time. Great things require a great investment of time, and the development of your personal power is a great undertaking that can and should last the rest of your life.

I suppose if you did want to reduce *Kung Fu* to one English word you might use *Mastery. Mastery* implies much more than the acquisition of a functional skill; it also speaks to experience and wisdom developed over *time.*

So, the ***Kung Fu Triangle*** contains the ***Dynamic Components*** of:

- ✍ **Motivation**
- ✍ **Discipline**
- ✍ **Time**

These are the components you'll use to *develop* power. Without understanding how *Kung Fu* works, the *Power Triangle* is pretty useless. It takes motivation and discipline over time to develop the skill you need to consistently apply balance, focus and timing to generate power and produce desired results!

The secret for using these components is ***practice.*** In fact, the *"ultimate secret"* of the martial arts is practice. Through practice over time you develop the ability or capacity to accomplish your goals. Isn't that a good working definition of personal power?

Earlier I said that an essential element of *Kung Fu,* often lost in translation, is the element of *time.* Try to buy into the idea that to achieve lasting and substantive success you'll need to commit to a sustained effort for a considerable period of *time.* This process of dedicated effort is more important than any particular result. That's a pretty heavy concept. In order to really appreciate this idea you're going to need a strong foundation, or *source,* of power.

The Energy Triangle contains the components that comprise the *sources* of power. The *Energy Triangle* contains the *Dynamic Components* that make us human. Each of these components represents an aspect of our human identity from which all human endeavors originate. These components, while difficult to quantify, form the substance of our life experience.

The ***Dynamic Components*** of the ***Energy Triangle*** and the *sources* of human energy and power are:

- ✍ **Body**
- ✍ **Mind**
- ✍ **Spirit**

I'm not going to discuss spirituality in a religious context; these ideas will fit into any particular religious belief. Frankly, your religious belief is your own business. I'll define *spiritual* as that which is difficult if not impossible to weigh, touch, see or taste. Spiritual realities are those we experience through our *feelings. Spiritual* defines the part of human experience we know to be real through our feelings, but exist outside our capacity to fully understand.

While we know *body* as a physical entity, I'm using this word in a metaphysical sense. The body describes our experience of the material self that supports human life; it's our tangible perception of the experience of human life.

We really don't understand the concept of *mind* without *body.* In Asian philosophy, any separation of the two is an illusion. Can the mind exist without the experience of the body? Yet, our mind can, through imagination, move far beyond the physical construct and limitations of the body.

Whew, that's pretty heavy! At any rate, our experience of body is through what we perceive as physical sensations and feelings. It provides our *tangible* connection to the universe. Until proven otherwise, you need to support and nourish the body to sustain a healthy mind and spirit. A healthy body requires exercise, physical challenges and stimulation as well as the rest, proper nourishment and relaxation.

Likewise, the mind needs stimulation and exercise as well as rest and relaxation to stay healthy. Some researchers have asked the question: does the mind produce the body or does the body produce the mind? Greater minds than mine will have to solve this problem. What's important to me is that the mind and body seem to be complimentary aspects of my human existence. What's really nice is that exercising the mind usually also benefits the body and vice versa; caring for body benefits mind and the other way around. This is yin, this is yang!

The *spirit* is the source of all natural power whether I understand it or not. *Spirit* can't really be intellectually experienced, it just is. If you are of a particular religious mindset you might say that your spirit is your gift from God without which life would not be possible. If you're agnostic or atheist, you might say that *spirit* is your inherent human identity, that which makes you uniquely human; the origin of which is beyond the range of human comprehension.

Mind is the source of all human experience. It's where your ideas come from. It's what makes you...You! The human mind is what makes us different from other living things, as far as we know. The mind is what knows that you exist, and wonders what to do about it!

Body, well that's your link to what might be called *reality* in Western thought. The body is the source of the tangible experiences of human existence. Your body gives you dimension and space in time. The body processes all external stimuli and most internal stimuli as well. As far as anyone knows, human existence doesn't happen without a body. The body is the source of human energy in the physical world. Take care of it, you don't get another one! *(At least this time around!)*

Before I get into the nuts and bolts I want to define some of the other terms I borrow from Asian philosophy. I don't use these terms to try to appear mysterious or distance myself. I use these words simply because there aren't any English words that have the same meaning.

You can see by now that *balance* is probably the most fundamental ***Dynamic Component.*** The idea of balance is often expressed in Asian philosophy through the terms *Yin* and *Yang.* Balance is a good word and will work just fine in our discussion most of the time. I'll also use the words *Yin* and *Yang* to express some ideas that transcend the limitations of the definition of balance.

Simply put, *Yin* represents the female, submissive, dark or deep sides of nature. *Yang* represents the male, aggressive, or light sides. What is particularly important to understand is that one cannot exist without the other; each is an integral part of the whole expression of nature or life.

The main reason I use these terms is that the *Yin and Yang,* particularly when pictured together in the iconic symbol familiar to most people, speaks to a dynamic quality of balance, or *harmony.* In this discussion balance is not static; balance is dynamic, ever changing and ever moving. As we experience life we must constantly adjust to these changes. This is the never ending experience of action in life. Balance in life means to live in relative harmony with nature and the universe. The only absolute constant in nature is change.

Just look at the *Yin and Yang or Taiji Symbol.* Doesn't it look as if it's moving? If the ancient philosophers meant to imply a static condition, they might have simply drawn a circle with a straight line down the middle!

Next is the word *"Chi." (Pronounce: "Chee")* In Chinese Philosophy 101 it would be proper to simply define *Chi* as energy. The Chinese would place this energy in context to indicate the source or manifestation of a particular energy. We all generate *human chi;* the binding energy of gravity would be described as *earth chi;* the life giving power of the sun would be *heaven chi* and so on.

I use the word *chi* because it can be applied across a broad spectrum of human experience. The word *chi* represents the life force that pre-exists our particular human experience. It's the energy that was generated by the union of our parents. It's the energy that allows you to self-generate from the moment of conception. It's the energy that manifests itself with every division of every cell in your body. It's also the energy you share with others as you develop and utilize your potential and your personal power.

Personal power is one manifestation of *chi.* Of course, that's the one I'm going to focus on in this book!

I may also use the word *"Kata"* from time to time. This word simply means *correct behavior. Kata* are the long choreographed performances practiced by martial artists. *Kata* is an exercise in perfection, usually based on a set of prescribed movements and actions.

I borrow this term from Japanese culture where nearly any activity done mindfully is *kata.* Many of you may have heard of the Japanese Tea Ceremony. This simple act of making and sharing tea is performed as an exercise in perfection. The Japanese understand that any activity practiced mindfully can become a powerful tool for self-development as well as a beautiful art form to share with others.

I want to make one more important distinction before we roll up our sleeves. I see an important distinction between what we call *principles,* and what we call *rules.*

Principles are unchanging, foundational truths. *Rules* can be changed, ignored, bent or broken. The ***Dynamic Components of Personal Power*** are *principles.* You need balance, focus and timing to express full power. You can't express full personal power without balance, focus and timing. Compromise balance, we get less power. Lose focus, less power. Conversely, pay attention to one of these components and you're likely to increase abundance and power in the others as well.

A rule might be "use the principle of balance in every area of your life." You can *bend* the rules! You might apply balance in business but not at home. You might achieve success in business, but still not be happy at home. Of course, you'll ultimately be happier and more successful when you create and apply a solid set of personal rules to govern and guide your behavior across the full spectrum of your life experience. The nice thing about rules, however, is that you can adapt and change them as you progress and develop, or to suit particular applications. Sometimes new and different rules are necessary at different times and places in our lives.

To enjoy true success and happiness, you'll need to develop and maintain discipline with an over-arching set of rules. That set of rules will be your ethical and moral compass. As far as I'm concerned, this falls into the *"your business"* category, as do your personal religious beliefs. I can say that if your ethics are in line with the natural tendency to promote human development and preserve life, your chances of true success are much greater. If your rules are out of synch with these laws of nature, you might achieve a great deal only to miss out on the ultimate expressions of human success: the love, respect and companionship of others.

It might help you as you work through ***Dynamic Components of Personal Power*** if you identify a single, significant goal. As you explore this process, you can apply the

Dynamic Components to a single tangible goal and track your progress.

Before you start the next chapter, take a few moments and identify one significant goal you would like to accomplish over the next year. Don't worry at all about how grand this goal may be. You can use the section in the "Power Drills" section titled "One Big Goal" for this exercise.

Identifying a significant, life changing goal will help you explore firsthand how to put the ***Dynamic Components*** to work. Working toward your *Big Goal,* you'll enjoy many small victories along the way!

How Power Works: The Power Triangle

In physics, power is how much work you do over how much time it takes you to do it.

$$P=W/t$$

Don't confuse power with *exertion*. Power is how you measure the result of your work; exertion is how hard you're working. In this formula, exertion is the "W."

You can work really hard for a short period of time and produce a burst of power. Or, you can work more efficiently over a longer period, producing the same power with less input energy. A device that produces the same or more power with less input energy is called a machine. One of the simplest machines is the lever. Use the ***Dynamic Components*** to create *leverage* in personal and professional life, and produce personal power efficiently.

Remember that our definition of *personal power* is: *the capacity to produce desired results.* Sometimes you'll want do put the pedal to the metal, but remember that to produce the same power in a shorter time requires more input energy, more *umph!* Most of the time in real life, you'll want to find ways to work *efficiently.*

Once you understand the *Power Triangle* you'll be able to produce personal power *effectively and efficiently.*

The ***Power Triangle*** contains the three ***Dynamic Components*** of:

- **Balance**
- **Focus**
- **Timing**

Let's break it down…

Balance

I'm going to spend some time on the component of balance. Notice I've placed *balance* at the base of the triangle. Balance is the foundation of the philosophy of the ***Dynamic Components.*** If you pressed me for the most fundamental component, I'd have to say *balance.*

Balance is the philosophical idea that nature favors harmony. Act in harmony with your nature and you'll be creative, productive, and feel a sense of ease; you'll be *going with the flow.*

Act in harmony with nature and you experience life as part of your environment and feel a sensation of belonging. You'll be part of the big picture and you'll have access to the power that's abundant all around you. You'll be well connected to the natural power of the universe.

A good sense of balance helps you manifest courage to offset fear. In fact, how would you even know courage without fear? Balance anxiety with confidence, complacency with action and obsession with forbearance. Pay attention to balance and you'll develop an instinctive sense that helps you recognize the opportunities in every adversity.

I purposely picked the word ***Dynamic*** for the title of this book and philosophy. Each component is *dynamic*, always fluid, adaptable and changing. Your success and happiness is directly proportional to your ability and capacity to manage that change and adapt to constantly fluid circumstances, conditions and opportunities.

In a dynamic sense, balance is your ability to create conditions of relative equilibrium in your life. I'm sure most of you would agree that success and achievement involve risk. Fear and anxiety can freeze you in your tracks and prevent you from taking risks necessary to your success. You'll need to continually balance fear by developing the courage to act in the face of danger and fear.

You'll also want to balance work and play. You need to balance the time you give to others with the time you spend cultivating your *self.* You need to balance tension with relaxation, and action with rest.

Without balance, focus becomes obsession. Without balance you might concentrate on the mind to the detriment of a healthy body. You might work so hard you sacrifice your life at home, or play so much you never get any work done.

Act in harmony with nature and other people in your life and you'll experience a much greater feeling of peace and prosperity. You'll connect with the sense of abundance that comes from the collective power of the universe and of the people around you. Connect with the power of the people you work with and you create powerful organizations.

I'm sure many of you are interested in developing personal power to increase material abundance. To be blunt, you might want to develop personal power to make more money!

Thomas J. Stanley, Ph.D. did an incredible amount of research to determine exactly how millionaires think. He focused on those who considered themselves wealthy and successful, emotionally as well as materially. Dr. Stanley starts his book, ***The Millionaire Mind*** with this observation of happy and successful millionaires:

"They live in lovely homes located in fine neighborhoods. ***Balance is their approach to life.*** *They are financially independent, yet they enjoy life-they are not 'all work, no play' type of people."*[9]

If you want to express power efficiently and effectively, balance is your starting point. Whenever possible initiate every action from a balanced position. If you're out of balance, take action to restore balance. Find activities that balance and compliment the extremes in life.

Balance is also your moral compass. When you act, how does that affect the people around you? How do your actions today affect your life tomorrow? When you take, is there something to give? When you give, is there something to receive?

We always see our lives and the world around us through the lens of human perceptions. At best human beings have a pretty limited range of perception. We only hear a small part of the full spectrum of sound and only see a small fraction of the full spectrum of light. Most of the time you're going to have to do the best you can and make judgments based on what you see and hear. Your mind, however, is not limited in the same way; you can extend your *"spectrum of understanding"* by expanding the potential of your imagination and intellect.

Mr. Newton understood an application of the component of balance when he said that every action produces an equal and opposite reaction. Keep the component of balance in mind as you act and you'll maintain philosophical and emotional grounding; in martial arts we call this *rooting* or *centering. Rooting* implies a solid foundation and a tendency to act in harmony with your nature, and the natural processes of the universe.

When you act from an unbalanced position, power is diminished. Action without balance can be weak and misdirected. If you express power without balance, there is the danger that your actions may violate your ethical boundaries.

In martial arts we are constantly trying to produce more power in a punch or a kick. Without balance, you could throw a punch with a tremendous amount of force yet miss your target, even fall. To produce results you've got to have your feet under you.

Without balance, power is wasted. Imagine throwing a punch as you're falling away from your target. You might work awfully hard and use a lot of energy, but the result is a weak punch: no power. Sometimes you'll have to fire a strike quickly without establishing perfect balance, but in this case you'll always trade off power.

In life, action without balance can become selfishness. People who act without balancing actions against consequences are usually the people we consider selfish and exploitive, even criminal or evil. They produce power without regard for how it will impact or affect others. They take without regard for resources. They demand without appreciation. They destroy rather than build.

Living a life without balance is very expensive. Ignoring some part of life, or your part in the lives of others, inevitably leads to stress, confrontation, illness, and poverty. It takes a lot more energy to live without balance. No matter how often you see someone exploit others for profit and seem to get away with it; there is always payment due in the end.

Truly successful people, on the other hand, understand balance and maintain relative equilibrium in material, emotional and spiritual life. Happiness and stress simply don't go together; to enjoy happiness you've got to reduce stress. The fact is that a life unbalanced by greed and exploitation is always under stress. Power that comes from fear and control always produces paranoia, and eventually poverty, in one or all areas of life.

People have the choice whether to cultivate and apply power for good or evil. Power, however, isn't in and of itself good or evil. These are just terms we use to describe the application of power based on a particular perception. Perception is relative to your capacity for understanding, as well as a product of the time and place in which you live.

The Chinese use the terms *Yin and Yang* to describe *negative and positive* energy. The *Yin and Yang Symbol* is made of two areas, one black and one white. Each appears to be moving into the space occupied by the other, yet each retains one small dot or portion of the other. Historically this symbol was developed from watching fish in a tightly stocked pond. The original symbol shows two fish, each swimming into the area just vacated by the other.

One of the primary philosophical meanings of this symbol is balance and harmony. This balance and harmony are dynamic and ever changing. Balance is not a static state, but a dynamic and constant interplay between what appears to our limited human perception as opposite forces.

This theory can be very simple to understand and apply to your life. As I said earlier, life is not static. Conditions, circumstances, opportunities and resources are constantly changing. You can develop and express much more power when you actively cultivate your skill, abilities, knowledge, and understanding to work in harmony with present conditions, circumstances, priorities and opportunities.

So, balance is not the absence of change. Balance is your ability to work in harmony with these dynamic forces to constantly create a happy and productive life.

The light area of the symbol is called *Yang. Yang* represents positive energy or potential for positive change. *Yin* is the dark area. This represents negative energy or direction. The natural condition of life depends upon the maintenance of a slightly more positive energy.

Of course, the positive energy is balanced by negative energy. Too much of either is not healthy. *Depression* is an extreme condition of a negative imbalance; too much positive energy and a person may be ignorant or blindly optimistic; at worst dangerously optimistic and at best annoying!

The trick is to recognize that negative and positive exist in nature and in life and, well, that's the way it is. Work in harmony with this natural order rather than trying to oppose it or swim against the tide and you create a more balanced and ultimately, more productive life.

This can be difficult, particularly when dealing with a lot of negative energy or circumstances. It's sometimes easy to get caught up in the negative, even unconsciously giving negativity more energy. It's more powerful to recognize the dynamic nature of the process and take action to prepare for, or expedite, the positive phase of the cycle.

In Chinese philosophy, *earth chi* is the energy that binds you to the ground. You might substitute the word *gravity.* When you work *with* this natural force you can maintain a well rooted stance. Work *against* this force and you create tension; you disconnect from your stance and the ground. Ultimately, if you don't understand how to work in harmony with gravity, you'll fall! The same idea applies in emotional and spiritual life.

What is the *"ground"* that supports your life? What is the *"earth chi"* that binds you to this stable and supportive ground?

Setting priorities and defining your key areas of life is a very personal process. I'm quite sure that for many of you, family would be a key area that can provide you with stability, rooting and balance. I don't have children, however, given my career, I might substitute teaching or coaching in place of parenting. As well as teaching martial arts to kids I'm a volunteer football coach. Whenever I work with kids I'm energized by their spirit and their willingness to learn. These activities provide solid ground for me emotionally and balance the rest of my work, which tends to focus on adult issues such as business and finance.

What are the key areas of your life? Some examples may be work, family, children, friendships, health, continuing education, church, volunteering, fitness activities, or hobbies. Make a list or a mind map identifying the most important areas of your life. You're choosing your ground, the foundation upon which you'll create balance in your life.

Here's a conundrum: In order to be rooted and work with this force that draws you toward the ground, you need to be relaxed! Tension is the enemy of rooting. Using the example of our martial arts stance, as you tense your legs, you're actually pushing yourself *away* from the ground. Relax and sink into your stance and you'll be well rooted.

In order to relax and still maintain a rooted stance you've got to condition your legs. To train, a martial artist spends a lot of time standing in deep, sometimes painfully deep, stances. In order to be well rooted and keep your balance, *you've got to develop strong legs!*

The *Key Life Areas* you identify are your emotional and spiritual legs. What can you do to make them strong? Your emotional and spiritual conditioning program must include whatever you need to do to take care of your *Key Life Areas.*

Self-improvement is the overarching activity that strengthens every key area of life. Your physical conditioning program should include cardio vascular, strength and flexibility training. Emotional and spiritual conditioning should include continual education, cultivating good personal relationships with family and friends, constructive and restorative leisure activities, and the practice of kindness, respect and tolerance.

Improve yourself in every key area of life and you continually strengthen your foundation and improve your balance. Any activity that improves or enhances your *Key Life Areas* strengthens your emotional and spiritual legs.

As I said, the enemy of rooting and balance is tension; tension wastes energy. The more tension you feel, the more energy you're going to expend. You'll become disconnected from your root; you'll exhaust your legs. Try standing with your back to the wall, and then slowly squat until your legs are bent at a ninety degree angle. How long can you stand this way? As tension creeps in, energy creeps out. ***Tension is very expensive.***

Properly expressed, balance is a state of ease and synergy. Preserve harmony between the key areas of your life and you'll work efficiently on any goal, and the other key areas will support your effort. If you set your sites on a promotion at work or want to start a business, consider how that goal will impact other key areas in your life. Who else is affected? Develop your plan to achieve your goal, and in that plan include activities that will balance all the important areas in you life. Include the people who will be supportive of your efforts; they provide your strongest base.

Ignore any *Key Life Area,* work without balance, and you'll eventually have an emergency to deal with. Emergencies happen when you have to suddenly switch your attention to an area of life you've been putting aside. All your *Key Life Areas* require care and feeding. When you ignore a particular area, it will eventually demand your attention, and probably with urgency! There's a lot less tension and fatigue when you constantly pay attention to balance and consistently pay attention to all the key areas in your life.

Emergencies are the well from which most tension springs!

Take a few moments and create a significant, life-changing goal. For now, you can let your imagination run wild. Don't worry about how realistic you might feel this goal is; simply pick a goal that you would really like to accomplish, and that would significantly improve your life in some way.

Write this goal on top of a page. On the left side of the page make a list of your *Key Life Areas.* Next to each, write a quick line describing how your goal might impact that area. Don't go into great detail, just jot down your gut feeling, or instinctive response about each.

Once you finish this exercise, look at the comments you made about how each area of your life might be impacted by your goal. For example, you might want to take some college classes required for a promotion at work. Taking college classes may decrease the amount of time you spend with your kids, but earning your degree may position you for a promotion at work which would help the family financially. Your new job may also be more personally satisfying, making you a better resource to your family and others in your life.

Think how your goal relates to each of your *Key Life Areas.* Label your comments *Yang* or *Yin. Yang* is for items having a *positive* impact in that area, *Yin* for those having a *negative* impact. A plus or minus symbol would work just as well. *You'll find a worksheet for this exercise in the "Power Drills" section titled "Balance Worksheet"; feel free to make some copies to use whenever you'd like.*

Once you understand how a particular goal will impact the key areas in your life, you have the information you need to make a decision from a position of balance.

You've labeled each item either positive or negative. Now think about each of these items and see if there's a negative side to a positive item, or see if you can find a positive angle in the case of a negative impact. For example, if a night college course takes some time away from the kids, a negative, you might all do homework and study time together turning that situation positive. You might look for ways to spend more time by including the kids when you go for a run or lift weights. You might find that you've got to adjust your schedule to create balance. The solution might be to spread classes out a bit while working toward your promotion, or if you decide the time is now, and you need to focus, you might solicit the support of your family by including them in your decision. Be open and honest about the potential consequences, both positive and negative.

Analyze each area of your life and see if this goal can be accomplished with relative balance. This is the beginning of the process of generating personal power. Caution: you *can* generate personal power without balance. The condition of power without balance is "obsession." Obsession is never healthy in the long run. The fact is that generating power without balance is an expensive drain on all your power resources, materially, emotionally and spiritually.

Working with the ***Dynamic Components*** requires *awareness.* Paying attention to balance is the key to developing goals that truly enhance life. Pursuing a goal mindless of the impact on other areas of life is usually wasteful at best, and in the long run can cause a great deal of tension, stress, pain and disappointment. Ultimately, your personal vision of success impacts the people around you. I'm sure when you realize your dreams; you're going to want some great people around to share your success with!

The greatest tools for maintaining emotional and spiritual balance are your personal values and ethics. For some, values and ethics are inherited. For others, it may be necessary to create a set of values and an ethical code.

Of course one of the ironies in life is that sometimes just when you think you're on the right road, that road turns into the highway to hell. Do the best you can with the information you have right now. Sometimes a goal that at first appears positive may produce a negative outcome. At other times our greatest triumphs come from what originally looked like a disaster.

It's important when thinking about balance to include the area of personal or family finance. I'm not qualified to write a book on personal finance. I recommend some wonderful resources in the "Continual Education" section on ***JimBouchard.org.*** I've learned through personal experience that some areas lie outside my talents and abilities; in these cases, I've learned to consult with experts. When it comes to finance, I'll refer you to the experts!

Finance is a very personal area and decisions in this area can be very emotional. Applying the principle of balance in finance makes seemingly complex decisions more obvious. Making out-of-balance financial decisions can lead to disaster. Just as with other areas of life, financial decisions can greatly impact other important people in your life.

Let's return to our example case, in which you're considering college classes to improve your position at work and make more money. Let's say you've identified "family finance" as a *Key Life Area.* What if money is tight right now? You might quickly jot down the comment that financial resources are scarce right now and label that as a *Yin* or negative observation.

A mitigating positive impact might be that even though earning this degree will be somewhat difficult financially, the potential earning increase, even over the next couple of years, will yield a very positive return. You might also find that by living on a tight budget during this time, you learn the value of careful planning and accounting. You may even develop a better system for saving you can apply in the future.

On the other hand…let's say that in doing your "Balance Worksheet" you find that even with a raise and new job, the increase in salary would be fairly modest compared to the money you'd spend on this degree. Or, you may simply not have the money to complete this degree at this time. What initially looked like a positive might start to look like a negative. That's OK; you considered the question with a balanced perspective and you'll make the right decision. The right decision is usually the one possibility that has the greatest probability for a positive outcome.

In business a similar exercise is the creation and review of a "Balance Sheet." This report shows the relationship of assets to liabilities. In a healthy company the balance sheet would be positive, or "in the black."

During this process discuss the options with your family, friends and trusted advisors. Putting your heads together, you may see a new opportunity, or a better way to achieve your goal. Earning this degree may position you to move to a new company or start your own business. You may decide you can find the money to make this happen, but suppose the timing is not right. Looking at the situation with a sense of balance, you might decide to take a part-time job to start saving tuition money, or start your degree on-line so you can spend more time at home.

Sometimes *inaction* can be your best course of action! Sometimes you have to stand fast to stay in balance. Once in a while the best action is not to initiate any action, at least for now. We'll cover this more when we talk about *timing*.

Of course sometimes you don't seem to have any choice. What about when catastrophe strikes? Every disaster is an opportunity. Of course, in my experience, it seems that nature has a grand plan to generously offer me the incredible opportunity inherent in crises when I'm least prepared, rather than when my life is in perfect balance!

There are also times when you're fully aware that the decision you're about to make is going to spin your life into turmoil, but the time is right; you've got to act now. So be it, you buckle your chin strap and step up.

Other times you'll assess the situation and despite some challenges in the short term, you see the long term rewards will far outweigh any hardships along the way. In this case you assess the risk and accept the challenges. The short term negatives of fear and failure can be balanced by determination, preparation and courage.

In all of these cases, the component of *balance* is fundamentally important. In fact, it's probably more important to pay attention to balance during when life seems to be most chaotic. At these times you've got to consider the longer view and see balance as part of the bigger picture. You may have to survive a period of imbalance as part of your long-term plan to establish lasting balance and harmony in life.

Later we're going to talk about the importance of *time* to the ***Dynamic Components of Personal Power.*** For now just try to keep in mind that sometimes you'll wobble, but you're not going down! Even the best fighters have to take a punch once in a while!

When times are tough it's useful to look at the punches you're taking as part of your master plan. Rough patches are the most fertile times for life lessons. Adversity demands creativity and opens your mind to new ideas and solutions. Sometimes losing creates a greater desire for winning.

Balance is a fluid and dynamic part of life. The secret is to understand and work with this dynamic flow to maintain an overall positive energy and perspective, even in times of trouble.

Ultimately, how you deal with disaster and opportunity is completely up to you. Keep this thought in mind throughout this book: ***the only person responsible for your success is you.*** I'm not trying to tell you what to think; I've simply come up with a system that helps me understand how power works and how I can develop power in my life. I'm trying to share this system, to the best of my ability, with the hope that it will help you develop and express personal power. This system is working well for me; I hope it works for you.

There are many systems you can incorporate into your personal success formula. I tell my martial arts students that I don't teach you a style, I teach systems. You can learn several systems of fighting; from those various systems you'll develop your individual style. You might say that a *system* is overarching and a *style* is what makes your expression unique. Style is your own personal expression of the system or systems you learn and incorporate. Eventually, you'll develop your own success *style.*

You have to decide exactly what constitutes balance in your life. I do know that you can only express personal power effectively and efficiently when you have a well developed sense of balance. Exactly how you create your sensation of balance is one of the many creative freedoms you'll enjoy as you work toward success.

I've learned from my life training in self-defense that there's no artificial practice scenario that will encompass every detail found in a real situation. No matter how realistic my practice is, I'm still aware that it's practice, not an actual life and death situation. It's very difficult to fully *practice* life and death situations. That's why the battle hardened warrior is best equipped to deal with adversity. The *Warrior* accepts life and death battle as an opportunity to test and perfect his skills.

Be the Warrior! Accept every challenge as an opportunity to practice creating success. Welcome adversity as an opportunity to test and hone your skills. When you embrace disaster *and* opportunity, you own the outcome. Accept personal responsibility for every challenging situation, and you also own the lessons each situation contains. When you understand balance as a *dynamic* principle, you naturally accept a little more risk, and enjoy a little more reward. Life is not static, it's dynamic!

As I said, sometimes it's best to stand fast, but stand still too often and for too long and life will pass you by. That's no life at all.

Apply the principle of balance and you'll be better able to find the opportunity in any disaster. Challenging situations provide practice in restoring balance. In moments of crises you learn to return to the positive flow of energy that's always available to you. You'll create goals that move you toward your greater vision of success, and you'll be much less likely to let problems detract you from your goals for very long.

Accept the risk and challenge of becoming responsible for your success and you're in a much better position to recognize and exploit the proverbial "opportunity of a lifetime." Some people seem naturally balanced when they're in very risky positions. *(Some of us feel really out-of-balance when there's no risk!)* Some of you may feel more balanced by taking your time, reducing exposure to risk and making sure resources are plentiful or timing is better before making your move.

The choice is yours. What I'm saying is that when you develop goals and make decisions based on the principles of the ***Dynamic Components,*** you'll develop a greater awareness of the energy and opportunity all around you. You'll become more aware of the abundant resources available to you, and you'll understand how to transform these resources into the power to achieve your goals. Your awareness, combined with your own experience, knowledge, and instinct will allow you to make the best decision in any given moment.

Keep the Component of Balance as the foundation of your planning. Understand that balance is dynamic.

Focus

The next ***Dynamic Component*** is ***focus.*** *Focus* is the ability to remain on task in a particular moment. You might say that *focus* is *the ability to be in the moment.* When you practice focus, your mind is clear, your thoughts are direct, and power is concentrated.

Back to physics: focus is the concentration of energy on a particular point. Let's say you can strike with 100 units of force per square inch, and your striking surface impacts an area of 10 square inches. What happens if you concentrate the same force into one square inch? The resulting power increase is tremendous!

In the application of personal power, focus is your ability to concentrate your energy, particularly your mental energy, on a particular task or goal. The potential of your mind is practically limitless. All the incredible accomplishments of mankind started when some individual, through the process of imagination, produced an idea and focused on the realization of that idea.

I'm actually just old enough to remember when going to the moon was a metaphor for impossibility. Someone decided it was possible, and a lot of great minds concentrated on making a trip to the moon a reality. The funny thing is that most of these great ideas are hatched long before the conventional wisdom of the time recognizes any realistic probability of success. You've got to start somewhere. When it comes to great accomplishments the first step is always an idea, a product of the mind.

Once you have a great idea, you've got to concentrate your mind's energy. You've got to *focus* your mental energy toward success. To do this you need a point upon which you can focus this mental energy. That point is a ***goal.***

We live in a very noisy world! How do you keep your mind on what you're doing in the middle of all this noise and confusion? Develop the skill of *focus* and you'll maintain a concentrated effort despite distractions, doubts and fears.

You could substitute the word *concentration* for focus when working on the mental aspects of this component. *Focus,* however, also speaks to proper attention to technique, coordination, accuracy and clarity.

Once again, don't confuse *exertion* with *power.* One of the masters I studied with used to ask this question: "Would you rather be hit by a BB gun or missed by a canon?" David knocked the Goliath senseless with a well focused strike. Focus is an important key in the transfer of input energy to develop maximum power. The BB might not have a lot of energy behind it, but a well aimed strike with the BB can, as your mother probably warned you, take out an eye! The cannonball might possess a lot of energy, but if it misses you'd consider yourself lucky. No result, no power.

In the business world, no serious advertiser commits financial resources to a campaign without identifying a specific target audience. One of the tools used to gather this information is a "focus group." Once a business establishes who is most likely to buy its goods or services, an efficient and effective campaign can be designed. Without focus, there's a great possibility of wasting valuable financial resources.

If I were teaching you a martial arts technique, I could isolate any part of that technique and begin the process of breaking down the lines and physics of the movement to maximize efficiency, and eliminate wasted energy. Let's do the same with any task or action that will bring you closer to the realization of your goals.

Focus is the quality of finding a quiet spot in the middle of all the noise and concentrating your mind's energy on a specific goal or task, in a specific moment.

Where is all this noise coming from? Negative voices make *a lot* of noise. When you decide on a meaningful goal, a lot of noise comes from people who are all too willing to tell you why you're going to fail.

Another source of noise is self-doubt. More noise comes from fear. Stress and worry make noise; still more noise comes from legitimate obstacles, and authentic and reasonable fears.

You have a choice, you can run around and try to shut off all the noise-makers, or you can learn to tune out the noise and find a clear channel in your mind. It's like the difference between listening to your favorite song on a scratchy AM radio station or in crystal clear digital audio.

It's much more efficient, and usually more effective, to train yourself to tune out the noise and tune into your potential. If the source of the noise is internal, like fear and self-doubt, you've got to practice self-motivation and discipline. Your clear channel is belief in yourself, and you're going to have to practice to develop a strong sense of self-belief.

If the source of the noise is external, like the voices of your detractors, you can sometimes turn the noise off at the source, or prevent it from becoming a problem in the first place.

I try to eliminate external noise in two ways. First, I only share my most important or risky goals with the people who believe in me and are willing to encourage me. I don't mean I surround myself with *yes men* who never offer clear, critical opinions. If I'm on the wrong path, I appreciate true supporters who have the courage to tell me so. What I mean is that I avoid people who lack knowledge in the area I'm pursuing, or those who have developed the self-defeating habits of procrastination, fatalism and laziness. I avoid those who cultivate negative attitudes and can't seem to wait to share that negativity with the world. I focus my attention on those people who are sincerely interested in my success.

I seek out people who have traveled the road ahead of me; their experience and wisdom means something. I seek out mentors who are adept at turning failure into opportunity. I want to hear from those who look at their failures as valuable lessons. I spend my time with people who will encourage me when times are tough and support me when I face my own doubts and fears.

Time, like mental energy, is used most efficiently when you focus your effort. I'm dedicated to success; I need to focus most of my time and attention on people who are successful and those who are, like me, trying to be.

When it comes to the people in our lives, it's not always easy to tune out the detractors. I find that I sometimes have to avoid sharing some of my goals with some of the people I truly care about. It's not always, or even usually, that the people who care about you are just trying to rain on your parade; they're usually well intended. The people who care about you don't want to see you get hurt. It's hard enough to stay focused on a major goal through all the normal trials and tribulations; you need to focus attention on those who are supportive of your efforts.

I know my own shortcomings and inadequacies well. I'm introspective and self-critical. I need people around me who will encourage my growth and help me see my potential. I need to focus my time and emotional energy on those who cultivate a positive attitude, and those focused on success and happiness.

If some people want to wallow in misery, that's up to them. I need to maintain my focus and not let their noise interfere with my music! If I have to spend time with a negative person, the secret is to appreciate the opportunity to practice staying focused on the positive in spite of being surrounded with negativity. The most challenging adversaries are sometimes our greatest teachers!

Focus depends on technique. There's a lot more power in a clean, accurate punch. Without focus you can certainly commit a lot of energy, but if your line is poor or you're off-target, most of that energy is wasted. If you miss your target, you might have worked very hard, but there's no pay-off, no *power.*

To develop focus, isolate a particular technique and practice with concentrated effort. Practicing this way you'll increase efficiency and eliminate waste. This works in personal and professional life just as well as it works in the ring.

How can focus help create power in business or professional life? The arts of commerce and selling are dependent on technique just as much as the arts of punching and kicking. Most of have sold something in our lives; I could make a decent argument to support the idea that *all of us sell something, some of the time!* Every time you try to make a point, you're selling. You sell when you go to a job interview, when you try to win an argument or when you're just trying to convince someone to let you have your way.

Most people have to sell something, at some point. Let's say it's my job to sell you a martial arts program; I'll use this example as I'm somewhat familiar with that process!

When I first started to earn a living as a professional martial artist, I was terrible at selling memberships; most martial artists start out as very bad salesmen. Most of us consider sales at best a necessary evil that allows us do what we really like to do: practice and teach martial arts. Fortunately, at some point I realized I needed to get better at sales if I were to survive.

I started to focus my effort on learning about the sales process. Early in my career I bought into the technique of telling a prospective student *everything* about my art and my classes on the first visit. I wanted to make sure that before he walked out the door, any prospective student would know exactly how much martial arts would benefit his life.

Unfortunately, I also made sure these prospects knew exactly how tough it would be along the way, how much pain they may experience and how much money it would cost them if they committed the rest of their lives to martial arts! I did a great job of talking many of them out of joining my program!

I created the perfect model of tremendous input energy producing very little power. I spent hours developing sales tools, flyers, price lists and flip-charts; my average initial meeting with a new prospect would last 20 minutes or longer.

Something I *did* do consistently over the years was to maintain focus on one over-arching goal: I wanted to improve my sales performance. For those of us who make a living providing a service, the development of new clients must be a primary goal. To survive, I knew I had to improve, and I stayed focused on my improvement.

I attended seminars, workshops and training sessions. I networked with other people who sold services. I studied books, videos and audio programs. I created my own "Dashboard University"; I'm sure I've logged hours worthy of an MBA degree listening to audio programs on the road.

Over time I learned to apply focus to my sales technique, just as I would when practicing a punch or a kick. I created goals that were more targeted; I created tasks that were better directed toward my goals.

At some point I became enlightened! What would happen if I simply asked the prospective student what he or she hoped to gain by studying martial arts? Again I'll point to the amazing Dr. Covey. Not that any one of his *7 Habits of Highly Effective People* are less important than the others, but one stands out among the rest as perhaps the cornerstone of personal effectiveness: "Seek first to understand, then to be understood."[10] The process of understanding someone else both demands focus and is, in itself, a practice in focus.

Once I was so enlightened, I simply started to ask prospects what personal goals they hoped to accomplish by joining my martial arts program. I asked parents what, if any, changes they hoped to see in their children. Through this process my sales technique became more focused and efficient.

One of the great blessings of life as a martial arts instructor is that I have never met anyone whose life could not be improved through martial arts practice. The process I learned and applied for success in my life as a martial artist can be used to help *anyone* realize *any* goal.

All I needed to do was to ask a question, and focus on the answer. I could then directly respond to the needs of my prospects. I focused my energy on helping the prospect attain his or her goals through martial arts. I stopped wasting my time and theirs with all the *noise.*

From that point forward I never had to sell a program again. I now enroll a new member in less than two minutes; an exponential improvement in efficiency! This is the power of *focus.*

Take a few moments and think of an area of your life in which applying focus would help you become more efficient and effective. Identify some key points and create some goals and tasks that will help you improve focus in that area.

As you work through this process, keep the first component of *balance* in mind as well. Be sure to analyze your goals and tasks in the context of balance in your life as a whole.

The art of focus is about tuning out some of the noise. In today's world, there's a lot of noise. There are a lot of people clamoring for your attention and you still have to face the daily grind of simply generating a living and taking care of your necessities.

Watch the news for ten minutes and you can get lost in the nail biting drama of world, national and local events. There are asteroids ready to obliterate the planet. Somewhere, someplace there's always a war on. Criminals are stalking, fires are burning, floods are flooding, and the cost of health insurance and gas just went up again.

If there's a moment of peace in all of this someone sneaks in an advertisement to tell you about something else you need right away, right now, today! It's a good thing someone shouted that need at you loud and clear or else you probably wouldn't even have know you needed whatever it was you now know you need!

This is an appropriate time to tell you that I don't preach from the ivory tower; I preach from the gutter! I'm one of the worst gadget heads you'll ever meet. I didn't know I *needed* High-Definition TV until I was *told* I needed it! Once I was told, that noise was a clanging bell in my head until I finally sat down to watch my first football game in *Hi-Def!* Then I knew that there is *some* truth in all that noise.

At any rate, it's hard to turn down the volume on all this noise. The good news is, it's simple, just not easy. It requires some discipline and of course it *requires practice!*

The best method to develop focus is *quiet meditation.* I'm not talking about retreating to a monastery in Tibet, though I would like to do that some day. Basic meditation is a simple process that can be practiced by anyone, almost anywhere.

Neither am I talking about meditation in a religious sense; I'm talking about simply taking some time out of a busy day to just *sit still and shut-up!* The key to turning off the noise is to focus on the fundamental and simple human process of *breathing.* Breathing is the most basic and natural process required by our bodies and our minds. It's ironic that we take so little time just to sit quietly and *take a deep breath.*

The health benefits of meditation alone are worth the investment in time and effort. Dr. Herbert Benson of the Harvard Mind Body Institute is one scientist who has identified a phenomenon he calls the "Relaxation Response."[11] Briefly, Dr. Benson found that spending time in some form of quiet mindful practice, with proper breathing technique, stimulates the immune system and improves our health. A quick search on the internet will produce pages of data relating to the benefits of meditation practice, including reduction of stress and anxiety.

There are hundreds if not thousands of techniques for meditation ranging from devoted religious practices to simple, quiet, breathing exercises. For our purposes I'm going to keep it simple. I encourage you to investigate this further.

The essential elements of an effective meditation session are these:

1. Find a relatively quiet place. An option is to put on some headphones with some quiet music.

2. Sit or lie down in such a way that your back will be straight and your breathing will be relaxed.

3. Breathe!

It really is *that* simple! Of course like any other practice, you can take meditation to some very profound levels. If you want to practice in more depth, I suggest you find a good teacher or access some of the resources available on our web site.

I teach a simple method of standing meditation and gentle exercise called *Qigong*. My video, ***The Energy Tapes: Basic Qigong,*** is available on-line at ***JimBouchard.org.*** In this video I teach a few simple sets of exercises that will do the job nicely.

To fully enjoy the benefits of meditation or Qigong, you need to practice a full, yet relaxed breath. This technique is called *diaphragmatic* or *abdominal breathing.* Simply put, you breathe by expanding your belly rather than your chest. This allows your lungs to fill to their most efficient capacity without tension.

Many people breathe from the chest. I've heard estimates that state that over 50% of Americans live in an almost constant state of hyperventilation caused by taking shallow breaths. A shallow breath doesn't bring in enough oxygen or get rid of enough carbon dioxide. In effect, a lot of people are slowly suffocating!

When you don't breathe properly you *hyperventilate*, or breathe faster to compensate. A full, relaxed breath is much more efficient and healthful. Medical data indicates that even one or two meditation sessions a day, of even five minutes, can improve your health and reduce stress. Aren't you worth five minutes a day?

Focus is a product of the mind. The most effective way to improve your focus and unlock your full mental potential is to meditate *mindfully.*

Here's a simple technique to get started:

Start a simple dialogue in your mind. As you breathe in, say "breathing in"; as you breathe out, say "breathing out."

Alternately you can slowly count, or pick a simple word or phrase, a *mantra,* to repeat again and again. The trick is to occupy the mind on something that does not require conscious thought. You're putting the conscious mind in park for awhile and letting the subconscious mind enjoy a natural and quiet state of simply being, *free from the noise.*

There are plenty of practices for developing focus. Chess, word games, learning a new language, and playing a musical instrument all develop focus. Reading, writing and stimulating conversation are also great activities for developing focus. You might join a reading circle or Toastmasters. You might take college or adult education classes or volunteer to teach others.

I never thought I'd live to utter this statement, but it now seems that even video games can improve mental skills, including focus! For years I've offered parents of my junior students the opportunity to donate recently purchased video game sets for use in a public demonstration of the destructive power of the Japanese sword. In other words, if parents are losing their kids to the video void, I offer to chop the games and consoles into tiny pieces.

James Gee and other researchers at the University of Wisconsin have conducted research that shows that playing video games can be "mentally enriching." In a special edition of *Discover* magazine titled "The Brain," Steven Johnson reported that Gee and other researchers "dared to suggest that gaming might be mentally enriching." While admitting that games might also be addictive, their study reveals that researchers "now recognize the cognitive benefits of playing video games: pattern recognition, system thinking, even patience. Lurking in this research is the idea that gaming can exercise the mind the way physical activity exercises the body. It may be addictive because it's challenging."[12]

I suppose I can now come clean about my secret addiction to *Madden Football* on *PlayStation.* It's comforting to know that when I'm playing *Madden,* I'm not goofing off; I'm improving my mental acuity!

However: playing video games *alone* is not going to improve your life. You need a *balanced* approach to exercise in body, mind and spirit to live a healthful life. Video games do *not* exercise the body, at least not as of this writing. On the other hand, sports and athletic activities *do* simultaneously exercise the body, mind and often the spirit. Mindful physical exercise can improve your capacity to apply all the components in the *Power Triangle: balance, focus* and *timing.* I'm probably inviting an argument, but I know from personal experience that competition improves my capacity to use every ***Dynamic Component*** in my life. That's part of the reason I still play football at middle age!

I admit more than a little bias, but practicing martial arts is one of the best activities you can do to cultivate personal power! You can choose from a wide variety of martial arts ranging from the gentle practices of *Tai Chi* to the hardcore combat arts of full contact kickboxing and mixed martial arts. Most of the professional martial art centers in America fall somewhere in middle, or offer a range of options within a particular center or system. My only specific recommendation is that you find a teacher who makes you feel comfortable. If you crave the extreme drill sergeant type of instructor who promises to torture you into becoming the complete warrior, so be it! There are plenty of instructors available with a kinder, gentler approach as well. In martial arts, there's something for everybody.

Before I move on there's one particular opportunity to practice and develop focus that also offers incredible long-term benefits for yourself and others: learning to *pay attention.*

You could say that focus is the *practice of paying attention.* I've heard it said that the greatest gift you can give another person is your attention. Paying attention to others is one of the greatest gifts you can offer the world, and it's one of the best ways to develop focus.

The most powerful technique for paying attention to s is mindfully listening. When you listen mindfully to the people in your life you're offering a wonderful gift, and you're strengthening your capacity to focus.

Sometimes people need to talk, when for you, it may not be the best time to listen. You might also find yourself listening to a topic of obvious importance to the other person, but you just can't seem to understand what the big deal is. Just as you'd add weight to a bar to develop more muscle strength, sometimes listening when you don't really feel like it, or when you're not particularly interested, can be a productive exercise in focus. Practice listening mindfully and attentively at these times and you'll increase your ability to focus. You'll also enjoy the added benefit of sharing compassion for another person.

There are times when you've got to protect yourself. You don't want to indulge emotional vampires, but as much as you can, and particularly with those close to you, try to pay attention as much as possible. Not necessarily for the reward, but simply because it's the right thing to do.

My purpose is to help you understand and apply the ***Dynamic Components of Personal Power.*** Understanding these components will help you generate and utilize personal power to realize your potential and goals.

Balance, and now *focus,* are two of these *Components.* I hope you can see how each is mutually supportive of the other. To fully express our potential, we must work in harmony with these basic components or principles. We must have balance in order to have a strong foundation, or support, from which to cultivate and express power. We focus our energy to express power effectively and efficiently.

Next we'll explore the most difficult component to master.

Timing

"If only I was at the right place at the right time!"

Have you ever used those words? You can have balance and focus, but without proper timing you'll produce little or no power! Timing is about knowing when to apply power to produce maximum results.

The Art of War is one of the world's most studied works on strategy. Written somewhere in the neighborhood of the 5th Century B.C., this classic is now considered required reading by military and business strategists in the 21st Century.

In *The Art of War,* Sun Tzu identifies 5 major keys to victory. The very first is:

"One who knows when he can fight, and when he cannot fight, will be victorious."[13]

Sounds like common sense, yet proper timing is probably the single most difficult component to master.

Returning to the lessons I've learned in the *dojo* I can tell you that you can develop some competency in balance with just a few weeks or months of training. Some skill in focus can be trained within a year or two of practice. Unless a student possesses some innate ability, *(and some do!),* it takes years to master timing.

Even the most skilled master constantly practices in order to maintain good timing. As strength, agility and speed start to decline, timing becomes the most important factor in combat, and for that matter, in personal and professional life as well.

Timing is the most *dynamic* component; timing is your ability to express power by executing technique at the proper moment. Timing is also your ability to read your opponent, or the conditions around you, in order to act at the precise moment you have the greatest advantage.

Sun Tzu offers us some more sound advice…

"In general, whoever occupies the battleground first and awaits the enemy will be at ease; whoever occupies the battleground afterward and must race to the conflict will be fatigued. Thus one who excels at warfare compels men and is not compelled by other men."[14]

Timing must be practiced diligently. Education and training are key areas essential to the development of good timing. Your sense of timing needs constant care and feeding.

My favorite martial artist is Muhammad Ali. I'm particularly inspired by what was probably his greatest fight, "The Rumble in the Jungle." *(If you like movies with a message I highly recommend* ***When We Were Kings****. Not only does this award winning documentary cover the personalities of everyone involved, but it's a great study of the politics and historical context of this incredible event.)*

Ali was the underdog. The "Rumble in the Jungle" was his shot to regain the championship against the much younger, and much stronger, George Foreman. Perhaps more than any other fighter in recent history, Ali was a master of timing. In a professional fight, timing is defined by the thousandths of a second that separates your opponent's punch from your slip or counter. It's the blink of an eye when a fighter deflects a blow rather than meeting it head-on, literally.

With proper timing, you command the ring, and to paraphrase Sun Tzu: *compel your opponent.*

Ali knew he had to compel Foreman away from his fight strategy. He trained to absorb the punishment George was capable of dishing out. He taunted, jibbed and jabbered at Foreman, psyching him into throwing everything he had throughout the first rounds of the fight.

At the precise moment Ali sensed that Big George was running out of gas, he opened up! The rest, as they say, is history.

George Foreman later became another one of my heroes and a great influence on my life. Many people would have been crushed by the kind of defeat George suffered at the hands of Ali. After the "Rumble in the Jungle," it seemed like Foreman was destined to be a footnote in boxing history; just one more of Ali's opponents on this path to immortality. He wasn't finished yet!

During some time away from the ring, Big George reshaped his life and reinvented himself as the successful, generous, and gregarious personality we know today. After a 10 year retirement, George embarked on one of the most incredible and improbable comebacks in sports history. His 1991 fight against the powerful champion Evander Holyfield showed every man in America that *there is life after age 40.* He lost that fight by one point but proved he was still a serious and viable contender. Then in 1994, at age 43, he regained the title by defeating 26 year old Michael Moorer.[15]

Today George is a successful businessman and entrepreneur. He's a minister, broadcaster, inspirational speaker, master salesman, and probably most important of all, a family man. He's a master of the component of *timing,* and he understands the value of perseverance and discipline. He knew when to walk away, when to restore himself, and when to come back. If you're serious about developing personal power, you've got to include his book, *By George,* in your library.

Timing in everyday life is no different than timing in the ring or on the battlefield. Develop skill in timing to maximize your chances to produce desirable results. To develop this skill you've got to train. Only constant practice keeps your timing sharp.

Of course, no matter how quickly you strike, your target may have other ideas; he may not want to get hit! In fighting, you can react quickly with a clean counter, but your opponent may act just as quickly and slip your punch. The better your timing, the more precisely you'll apply force at the exact moment for greatest impact.

Timing is also the ability to recognize and exploit opportunities. You've got to have good timing, but you also need the ability to recognize opportunity. A good sense of timing won't do much good if you don't have the tools and resources necessary to act when the time is right. You've got to *know* when to hold 'em, and *know* when to fold 'em! Knowledge and experience become important factors in developing and applying good timing.

The foundation of knowledge is education. Just as we identified *perfection* as a process, *education* is a process; it is part of the process of perfection. Constantly improve your base of knowledge. Strive to learn as much as you can in as many areas as possible. The time is *always* right to add to your store of knowledge.

Learning isn't restricted to traditional attendance at a school, college or university. In this age we all have unprecedented access to information in almost infinite form. Most local bookstores feature reference, self-improvement, psychology, and business sections the equal of most college or public libraries. If your bookstore or library doesn't have what you're looking for, just click Amazon, Borders or Barnes & Noble on-line. The internet also provides gateways to colleges, universities, libraries, museums, news agencies and other educational resources around the world.

If you want a formal degree or course of study, you can now even earn complete college degrees on-line without ever leaving your desk.

We now have video, computer learning programs, compact disks, MP3, and Podcasts. I'm sure by the time you're reading this book, many of these media formats will have been replaced by other, more efficient ways to store and communicate information.

There's no shortage of access to learning material. What you have to guard against is poverty in your will to learn! There are times in life when it may feel as if you're spinning your wheels; those times often contain the potential for the greatest change in your life.

My career as a martial artist really started taking shape after I was laid-off from a job as a producer at a television station. Before I was laid off, I didn't have time to train seriously in martial arts. I was also a professional musician at that time. Having been laid-off, I could have wallowed around in self-desperation, and honestly, I had my moments! Instead, I decided to invest most of my time studying and practicing to become a better musician and martial artist. I learned about business by managing my band; eventually I applied this business knowledge to martial arts and started my own school.

During this time I became a self-improvement education junky. I consider self-improvement and success genres pleasure reading. I am a voracious student of history. I enjoy reading and watching programs relating to philosophy, physics, science and nature. The better informed I make myself, the more enjoyable life is and the more tools I have to recognize opportunities.

I buy and download audio books and other audio and video educational materials. I named the sound system in my vehicle the "Dashboard University." I enjoy taking classes. I continue to study and learn about my interests including music, martial arts, business, philosophy, and of course, football.

The point is that I never know when knowledge from one source will lead to success in some other endeavor. I told you at the beginning of this book that the information I'm sharing with you now came largely from my interest and study of martial arts. My interest in martial arts opened for me, a fascination with the philosophy and culture of China and Japan. Interest leads to knowledge which opens new areas of interest.

Learning about martial arts, philosophy, football, and music has helped me develop powerful tools for my business, professional and personal life. I cannot count the times when some bit of information from philosophy or history helped me in a business deal, or at least kept my eyes and ears open to new opportunities.

Timing is about pulling the trigger at the instant you acquire your target. Knowledge is your ammunition.

Much of what I've learned in life has come from listening to and engaging in dialogue with other people. Having some knowledge in a wide range of interests allows me to converse with people who have the knowledge I'm looking for. Having a good base of knowledge enables me to understand what people are saying to me. Constant learning expands my ability to understand new concepts by relating them to similar ideas within my base of knowledge.

I think you get the message. An important element in developing personal power is to learn, continue to learn and learn more. Timing is a direct product of your ability to recognize opportunity and that ability comes from, and is a result of, learning.

The ability to act with proper timing is trained through experience. Knowledge doesn't always come from books. The most valuable learning, in a practical sense, comes from experience.

Experiential knowledge depends on how well you develop lessons from circumstances and conditions in which you find or place yourself. You can learn from success, and you can learn from failure. One of the most profitable experiences, if you know how to learn from it, is failure.

Everyone fails. My study of success has revealed this incontrovertible truth:

Successful people fail much of the time!

The trick is that successful people develop an intimate understanding of one of the most powerful components of power: discipline. Discipline is the development of the habit of repetitive mindful practice and perseverance.

There's an old saying in Korean martial arts, "Knocked down seven times, get up eight!" You'll probably fail a number of times on the road to any success, but success is built on the ability to learn from these failures and continue toward your goal armed with better knowledge.

I'll remind you again of my boxing trainer, Dave, "You always learn more when you lose!" Of course this philosophical gem was most applicable as I reflected on my loss with cotton stuffed up my broken nose after losing a fight!

Dave always left a pregnant pause after sharing this bit of wisdom, and then added, "But some days you don't want to learn anything!"

He was right! When we win, we may tend to congratulate ourselves and move on. When we lose, we usually spend some time wondering why.

Tom Brady and Bill Belichik of the New England Patriots are great examples of people who seek to learn from experience win or lose. Watch a Patriots press conference without knowing the score and you might not be able to tell whether the Pats have just won or lost. Win or lose, both of these men usually talk about what lessons they'll take from this game and what they're going to work on in order to improve.

This attitude may be the number one reason the Patriots, as of 2006, are considered the class of the NFL, and as of this writing, have won 3 Super Bowls in 5 years.

There's a time to reap, and a time to sow. Reaping is time spent in action and producing results; sowing is time spent cultivating and nurturing. Productive action is a result of good timing. Good timing is a result of cultivation, training and learning.

It's sometimes painful to be self-critical and take a hard look at our mistakes. Practiced with discipline, self-examination becomes energizing and restorative. There's nothing more exciting than improving your *Self.*

Learn when it's time to act and train to act in the right time.

A quick review:

The ***Dynamic Components of Personal Power*** are diagramed in 3 triangles, each containing 3 components.

The components of the ***Power Triangle*** identify how power is manifest or applied effectively. These components are:

- **Balance**
- **Focus**
- **Timing**

Use the *Power Triangle* like a lens or a prism. You can use it to understand exactly what you need to do to apply power effectively. You can use it to break power into its component parts and analyze whether or not it's the proper time or place for action.

To generate maximum power, act from a position of *balance,* and *focus* your energy at the proper *time.*

Be relentless in your search for knowledge. Dedicate yourself to developing the skills you'll need to apply these components in your thoughts and actions.

The key to unlocking human potential and creating your personal vision of success is to develop and apply your personal power. The more power you can produce the greater your potential to achieve your goals and create success.

"The best thing we can do for others is to constantly improve ourselves!"

Cultivate Personal Power and you become a much greater resource to the world, and the people around you. Happiness and success is in direct proportion to your ability and capacity to express personal power. It's your ethical and moral obligation to use this power to improve your life and the lives of others.

It's your nature to be powerful!

Before we move along...

I've got a secret for you. In fact, this is the *ultimate secret* of all martial arts. This secret has been around for thousands of years and has never changed. In my humble opinion this is the greatest secret to success ever discovered by mankind:

***The secret is*: PRACTICE!**

You simply cannot become expert without practice. You cannot master a skill without practice. You're going to have to practice to make the ***Dynamic Components*** work in your life. In the next chapter I'm going to talk about how this is done through the Components of the *Kung Fu Triangle.*

Practice produces experience. I've always found it interesting that a student must graduate from years of training to *enter* a practice in law or medicine. Practice is ongoing and never-ending. Practice is the *process* of perfection. Practice is not where we're going, it's where we are! It's not what we're *going to do*, it's *what we do!*

Knowledge and experience are part of the same whole, just as *Yin* and *Yang* are inseparable qualities of the one *Tao* or *Way*. Knowledge provides access to experience; in experience there is learning. This process is not a straight line; it's an ever expanding circle. Eventually, the result is *wisdom:* one of the greatest treasures you can share with others, now, and for generations into the future.

The Kung Fu Triangle

In the 1970's, *Kung Fu* was the name of a popular television series that inspired a generation of American kids to study martial arts. It's also a common term used in the name of some Chinese martial arts systems.

Kung Fu literally means *achievement through great effort.* This literal translation from Chinese language, however, falls short of the full meaning of these words.

My understanding of *Kung Fu* is expressed in the three *Components* of the ***Kung Fu Triangle:***

- **Motivation**
- **Discipline**
- **Time**

"Kung" is also sometimes translated as work. Motivation and discipline are the basic elements of work. To really complete the true meaning of *Kung Fu,* however, we've got to add another component: *time.* Motivation and discipline can help you gain skill; *mastery takes time.*

The component of time is always lurking in the background of the old martial arts stories and legends. In traditional cultures elders are revered and valued for their life experiences. They possess something everyone should value: *wisdom. Wisdom* only comes with experience, over time.

You don't completely achieve what the Chinese call *Kung Fu* through motivation and discipline alone. Your effort needs to be sustained over time. You might say that motivation and discipline are the elements of proficiency. Applying motivation and discipline over time is required to develop *mastery.* The concept of *Kung Fu* is always related to mastery above and beyond basic proficiency.

Developing personal power requires a lot of practice. In order to sustain your practice you're going to have to find some motivation. Then you'll need to develop discipline to sustain your effort over the long haul, when motivation wanes. When you're hot you're hot, when you're not, you need to be disciplined.

In your quest for personal power, you want to be a pro, not an amateur! As you go through this process, promise yourself that you'll make the application of the ***Dynamic Components*** a consistent practice in your life.

If you stop practicing just when you get it right, you're not as likely to keep going when things get tough again. If you keep practicing until you can't get it wrong; you'll stay busy practicing for the rest of your life.

Motivation

Motivation is whatever you welcome into your mind that compels your body to work. Motivation ignites action. Motivation is the spark that fires the engine of achievement.

Motivation in the human mind is a product of establishing goals. To achieve any desired result, you've got to apply your power to a particular end. Your overarching goal might be your personal vision of success. Your global vision of success is realized when you face challenges and prevail through trials.

In order to achieve great things you've got to find, face and triumph over a course of never-ending challenges and trials? Yes! This is life! Life without challenge is stagnant.

The component of *motivation* is the spark that gets you started. Somewhere, someplace you've got to find the spark. No spark, no fire.

Motivation can sometimes be external. A friend may turn you on to a new experience. You might be moved to action because of what your parents taught you, or because you met someone famous who ignited your inner passion.

The legendary singer Bobby Darin was motivated to become a star when he saw a Frank Sinatra poster outside the Copacabana nightclub. At that moment, he determined to play the same stage, and become just as famous as his idol.

Sometimes your spark comes from necessity. You may recognize a necessary or worthwhile task, and simply take the bull by the horns because you know something has to get done.

Sometimes the spark comes in a moment of crises. As a martial artist I strongly believe that every disaster is an opportunity. Allow crises to motivate rather than paralyze you, and you may become a hero! The greatest heroes always rise from the greatest disasters. Challenges and trials are the stuff from which heroes are made!

Challenges and trials can be quite enjoyable. In my life, martial arts provided quite a few challenges and trials. Martial arts practice obviously requires a lot of effort. It's sometimes frustrating, humbling, exhausting and painful. It's also one of the most enjoyable experiences I've ever had. I've had so many moments of great joy in my martial arts life that I can only being to hint at some of them in this book.

These challenges and trials helped me develop my *internal ignition system.* My *internal ignition system* now helps me better identify particular challenges and trials that lead to success. I've found that most of the time, challenges and trials synergistic with my larger goals tend to be the most enjoyable.

I'm often asked what initially motivated me to start practicing martial arts. I began my life as a martial artist because I had very little self-confidence, self-awareness or sense of self-worth. I *did not* feel worthy of respect from others, I *did not* feel worthy of recognition. I *did not* feel worthy of love. I really wanted a meaningful relationship, but my self-doubt created a self-imposed isolation of sorts. I became lonely and withdrawn.

Hindsight being 20/20, I can now see that I always had opportunities all around me, always. My problem was that I was wearing very dark glasses most of the time.

I became depressed. Thankfully throughout this period I remained open to the help of some very special people around me. I had some inkling of what I'd later understand as *Beginner's Mind.* I kept a somewhat open mind to new ideas and a somewhat open heart to the people willing to help me.

No matter how depressed or desperate you may become, you always have a choice; always. You can sink into deeper depression and eventually even destroy yourself; or, you can look for some *spark,* some *motivation,* that inspires you to take your first step in the right direction.

My brother Walter had been telling me about martial arts for some time. He probably doesn't even remember telling me about martial arts, and it's been years since he was involved in the arts. He was, and is, a hero to me. He was a martial artist, a Marine and a boxer. He's now a successful financial advisor.

This spark of interest in the martial arts he ignited kept flashing in my mind. After that, I probably started to pay more attention to old martial arts movies on TV. Asian philosophy had always fascinated me, but I now seemed to notice more opportunities to view Asian art, or to learn about Asian history or culture. It now seemed as if the bookstore shelves were full of books on martial arts and Asian philosophy.

About this time I can remember a particularly lousy day. I was working at a television station at the time. I should have looked at this job as one of the best in the world. Instead I looked at my job as a pain in the ass! At the time my dream was to become a full-time professional musician, but my band was struggling.

Just to make things more interesting the girl of my dreams broke up with me. My vision of myself was unattractive, and I cultivated my look to propagate that self-image. Despite a decent paying job, I was broke. My apartment was typical of the depressed twenty-something self-loather; full of empty spaces left when my girlfriend took her furniture and belongings. She also owned our only car. *I was now a broke, depressed twenty-something American male with no wheels!*

Depressed yet?

As if this weren't enough, it was time for my job review at the TV station. Since my boss was also a good friend, I thought I'd go through the cursory quick job review and be back at my desk in ten minutes.

Instead, my boss, Gordon, had a surprise for me. He told me in no uncertain terms that my job performance had deteriorated; if I didn't develop a more positive attitude, he'd have to let me go! How about *that* to brighten my outlook on life!

I thought about what Gordon had said and after initially getting angry, *I decided he was right.* Gordon was, and is, a man I greatly admire. His opinion meant something to me.

The fact that I thought Gordon was right probably still originated from a lack of self-worth, but that's incidental. The point is there was a *spark,* some *motivation.* It was now up to me to determine whether or not I could fan the spark into a flame and take the necessary action to change my life.

My brother's stories about boxing and martial arts ran through my mind. He had kept telling me martial arts could change my life, but I hadn't worked out in years and my health and fitness levels were atrocious.

I took a walk.

About three blocks from my apartment was a building with a massive sign that read **"KARATE."** What the hell, I walked in. Up a long flight of stairs I found another world. There were two students practicing throws. Bodies hitting the hollow wooden floor reverberated like the beat of Japanese war drums. I was quite impressed by the action on the floor, and the cool looking uniforms and thought to myself, "this is what I'm looking for!"

So…I walked out!

Motivation is a funny thing. First of all, it's only the beginning of our efforts, just the spark. If you don't fan that initial spark the kindling won't start. If you don't get a little flame going, you'll never build a fire.

A lot of caring people were trying to help and motivate me. I know now that they saw great potential in me, *but it was up to me to make to take the initiative.* Could I accept these challenges and trials as motivation? Would I allow these people to spark my inner fire?

You can be motivated, to a degree, by people and events around you, but ultimately you're the one who has to take the first step. All motivation must at some point be internalized. Internal motivation is always the most powerful.

It's also up to you to keep stepping for the rest of your life; "*Every journey of a thousand miles begins with the first step.*"[16] Take the first step, then another, then another.

In my martial arts journey, the first step I took was back down the stairs! Fortunately for me, the *Sensei* bounded out of his office and called from the top of the stairs. He said, "Come on in, I'll show you around!" Before I left, Dick Roy Sensei had me set to go with a uniform and a month of lessons.

A great ending to this story might be "and the rest, as they say, is history." For now I'll say that this is only the beginning!

That's what motivation is. It's the beginning. If someone else generates a spark for you, great! If you can find some spark from a movie, a book, a profound quote or anecdote, wonderful. If you see someone who is doing what you aspire to do, fantastic!

When you can take that spark and fan the flame, better. When you learn to recognize or develop a spark within yourself, best!

To recognize the spark you need an open mind and an open heart. In martial arts we try to develop an attitude of openness throughout our practice, throughout our entire lives.

This openness to new experiences, new learning and inspiration is called ***Beginner's Mind.***

For now I want to leave you with the understanding that whatever it takes to get you moving is called *motivation.* It's the spark that ignites your passion or causes you to take the first step in your journey. This spark can come from within, or ignited by an external source. It moves you toward your first step.

The next step is Discipline.

Discipline

It's easy to confuse *discipline* with pain, sacrifice and punishment. The opposite is true. Embrace self-discipline and you'll open your heart to the expression and enjoyment of your true passion and calling. *Discipline* is reading the compass that always points toward your goals and staying the course when motivation wanes. Develop self-discipline and your work takes on a flow and a sense of purpose, enjoyment and competency.

The ancient sage Lao Tzu says,

"Plan the difficult when it is easy;
Handle the big when it is small.
The world's hardest work begins when it is easy;
The world's largest effort begins where it is small."[17]

Discipline involves handling the big stuff when it's manageable, day by day. Discipline is developing the habit of constant attention; constant attention to the details, the goals and the tasks that will further your development. The earlier in life one develops this habit, the better.

Pay constant attention and you become focused; you do the work you need and want to do. Discipline keeps mind and body focused on your goals. With discipline you produce results; you manage small tasks, day by day, step by step, toward your ultimate vision of personal success.

If you lack discipline, you put off important tasks that may not feel exciting at the time. You put off work that feels like drudgery. You put off until tomorrow what you could have done today. Lack of discipline is a vacuum. Life never remains empty for very long; complacency and procrastination are waiting to fill the void.

When you procrastinate, minor details expand into disasters. Complacency transforms small tasks into burdens and emergencies. Tasks that are put off become items on endless to-do lists that never seem to get done. Eventually, the procrastinator becomes the whiner.

As Zorba says, "God gave us hands to grab with." Take the bull by the horns. Any goal, within the scope of your talents and abilities, no matter how impossible it looks at first, can be transformed to success by organizing and embracing a smaller series of tasks, and accomplishing them in timely fashion.

There is tremendous freedom in self-discipline. Unfortunately, too many people today equate freedom with a *lack* of discipline.

The contemporary sage Kris Kristofferson wrote:

> ***"Freedom's just another word for nothin' left to loose,***
> ***And nothin' ain't worth nothin', but it's free."***

He's right about that! Nothing ain't worth nothing!

You really don't have freedom just because you don't have any options left. A lack of options is the most abject form of poverty.

There's never freedom in scarcity. Freedom comes from abundance. If you lack discipline, you're bound to the graces of someone else for safety and security. You've got to ask permission before you take action.

Freedom is opportunity and choice; freedom is *realized* through discipline. Through discipline you become the true master of your own destiny.

Discipline is training your eyes to see opportunity. Discipline is training the mind to create solutions. Discipline is training the body to take action.

Lack of discipline causes worry, anxiety and stress. Think about the feeling you might have when the deadline is approaching for some major report. Let's say you've had six months to compile data and write this report; you're now facing the final week and you haven't started yet. How big is the task now? What if you had the discipline to pay attention to this task constantly throughout the past six months? A disciplined person might face the final week with only a couple of minor tweaks. The disciplined person is free to spend time refining and improving the final product.

Nearly all of us have procrastinated, at *one* time in our lives, when preparing our income tax returns. In fact, the cultural mythology surrounding this little two page form has reached such magnitude that many people are terrified of even the sight of Form 1040. An entire industry thrives on our fear of income tax preparation!

Any person with average math and bookkeeping skills, who earns simple income as an employee and owns one home, can probably fill out a form 1040 in less than hour. You could cut this time in half by using software or websites available to anyone with access to a computer.

Imagine how easy it would be if you paid constant attention and kept your records organized on a daily, weekly or even monthly basis. A disciplined person can literally answer a few interview questions on the computer and finish the whole terrible business in a few short minutes.

Discipline is the foundation of *Kung Fu.* Without discipline you may win once in a while, but only by chance. Jackpots aren't accomplishments, they're accidents. I won't pretend to be naïve, I wouldn't turn down a big lottery jackpot, but I also know that winning a pile of money doesn't create any feeling of achievement. Winning a prize only makes you feel lucky, *for now.*

Why do you think so many people end up broke after winning the lottery or scoring big at the casino? If most lottery winners possessed any self-discipline before they scored their jackpots, they would be set for life. Most truly wealthy people are not compulsive gamblers, and few of them play the lottery. They appreciate the rewards that came from hard work and are a lot less likely to risk their resources carelessly.

Some people are frightened of discipline. They know that it's hard work to develop self-discipline. They also know that discipline sometimes requires delayed gratification, doing without in the short term in order to enjoy greater benefits in the long term.

If you're afraid of discipline, become more afraid of leaving the important details of your life to chance. Develop discipline and *you're* in charge. Discipline is the foundation for developing the habit of success.

Discipline doesn't make you immune to failure. Even people that work hard experience failures; however, great success is often born of failure. Discipline is the habit of staying on course so that failures become paving stones for your road to success.

Developing discipline is simple; it's not easy! Yes, this again! To develop discipline you just need to identify a goal, start working on it, and keep working on it until you succeed. When you fail, keep going; when you succeed, repeat the process.

Simple, not easy!

Discipline and motivation are closely related. *Motivation* is whatever gets you going, and *discipline* is training yourself to keep going, even when you're not as motivated. The more discipline you develop, the more success you create. Success in turn rejuvenates motivation and the cycle begins again.

To develop discipline, it's better to start early, and it's best to start with something you love to do. *Make sure your children start early, get them involved in martial arts!*

One of the most incredible experiences you can provide for a young person is martial arts training. At any age, the martial arts provide a continuing and escalating series of challenges for mind and body. Progress in the martial arts is earned through constant practice and discipline. There's also no better training for balance, focus and timing.

Most martial arts programs provide a built-in system of motivational recognition. You might say you don't need recognition, or that the work itself is the reward, but it sure doesn't hurt to be recognized for a job well-done. The trick is not to be attached to recognition, or allow the opinions of others to be your sole or primary motivation. Still, recognition is useful in that it shows you that you're moving forward and that you're on the right track.

The human psyche programs us to seek pleasure and avoid pain. Sometimes daily life and tasks can be painful, boring, or unfulfilling at a particular moment. Recognition makes a powerful psychological connection between hard work and achievement, accomplishment and self-worth. When we're recognized for our efforts, our path to discipline becomes more sustainable.

Seek out activities that demand discipline. Look for work and play that offer some rewards in the form of recognition. Martial arts certainly fill this order; recreational sports provide opportunities in this area as well. Today there are opportunities for nearly everyone to enjoy athletics and sports from cradle to grave!

I continually seek out opportunities to test myself and practice discipline. The act of writing this book is one such exercise. As of this writing I'm 46 years old, still active in martial arts practice and I play full-contact football in a semi-professional league with men half my age!

Many people consider me crazy for indulging my football obsession, and I freely admit it *is* an *obsession!* I'm a life-long fan, but I never played organized football until age 44. My original intention was to be a kicker; actually my original intention was to indulge my mid-life crises. *(I'm not really into sports cars!)* At any rate, I also ended up playing free safety and occasionally punting.

One of the greatest things about a team sport is one's accountability to others. Accountability is a great motivator; in football, accountability to your team mates may be the prime motivator. If I don't commit myself to my job, I'm letting down every other man on the field. There is great truth in the phrase "football is the ultimate team game." Every man must do his job for the team to function effectively as a unit.

Even as a reasonably successful person of middle age, playing football and being accountable to a team helps me practice discipline, and provides an opportunity for recognition. I don't think I'm revealing any great secret when I say that every weekend warrior, in every recreational sport, wants to be a hero. The Saturday night touchdown might be the brightest spot in any player's week.

Even though football is a recreation in my life, it is important to me in many ways, and the benefits I enjoy from playing football translate into every other aspect of my life. The Saturday night touchdown, or in my case, field goal, injects a shot of positive energy and confidence into the following week's schedule at home and work, as well as on the field.

We all have times when it's difficult to muster up enough energy to be disciplined. In my first year of football I suffered a serious leg injury. I was punting; the snap from the center was off the mark and I had to scramble to control the ball. I saw that I couldn't get the punt off and started for a clear lane to the first down marker. I felt a tug on the back of my shoulder pads and a quick, sharp burst of heat across my right leg, just above the ankle. As I went to the ground, I watched my foot circle back and fly up toward my backside from a pivot point which was not my knee!

Before I hit the ground I knew my leg was broken. I had a compound spiral fracture of both the tibia and fibula. The tibia had broken the skin. The end result was that my tibia had exploded into a dozen or more pieces. Of course, this provided and endless supply of ammunition to those who delighted in telling me how crazy I was to play in the first place!

This probably should have been the end of my football obsession, or at least my career as a player. It turned into one of the greatest opportunities of my life.

I had a great support system. My wife and business partner, Alex, is also a talented personal trainer. She would see to it that the business ran smoothly and would take charge of my rehabilitation.

I was also blessed with the services of Dr. Stephen Rodrigue, whose experience included work with the New England Patriots: Perfect! His prognosis was that my injury was serious; *and,* that if I wanted to, he'd have me put back together and playing football next season!

Perhaps more than at any other time in my life I had to access the power of self-discipline that I had continually preached to my students. My recovery was painful, slow, and at many times very difficult. I dedicated myself to my daily training and accepted, (most of the time), that progress must be methodical and healing would be slow.

I accepted recognition from my supporters when they noticed that I was improving. This may have been the first time in my life I sincerely and gratefully accepted the praise and admiration of others. Sometimes it is hard to see the forest for the trees. In these times we should trust the eyes of those with a better vantage.

I had several very dark and discouraging moments and some set-backs, but I stayed focused on my goal to play football, at least once more, and simply kept at my training, on good days and bad.

Less than a year later I was playing again. I focused on becoming my team's place kicker. Some days I kicked well; other days I felt like kicking myself in the butt! Many days were frustrating, every day was painful. Kicking field goals demands precision and accuracy and results are readily measurable. I charted my kicks and while I made continual progress, failures were also well documented.

While I still had a long way to go, I was ready for our first game. I finished the season as the top kicker in our league, and helped my team to finish as runner-up in our division. In our final game, the division championship, I kicked 3 field goals on 3 attempts, including a forty yard kick that put us ahead late in the game.

My coach nominated me to the league All-Star team a week before my 46th birthday. Also selected was one of my best friends, our long-snapper Smokey Hicks: age 50!

I succeeded in this challenge largely due to the discipline I developed through martial arts training. I also recognize that the discipline I practiced in getting myself back on the football field strengthened me in mind, body and spirit. My sense of discipline was tested and magnified through this challenge. My new and improved sense of discipline and self-achievement now serves me in business, and all the other areas of my life. A lot of the motivation for writing this book came from this experience. *All this from getting myself mangled playing a stupid kids game in middle age!*

In business and professional life, discipline is essential to success. I've started several small businesses, some are succeeding, and some have failed. Even my successful business ventures have often been difficult.

Most entrepreneurs can probably identify with my experiences. Getting any business up and running is, to say the least, a challenge. In a small business, one or two people may be doing all the work. Working for yourself provides great freedom, but also carries great responsibilities. Sometimes revenue is scarce and bills are plentiful. In your own business you sometimes wake up as the CEO, have lunch as the salesperson, finish the afternoon as the janitor, and spend the evening as the accountant.

Any business is subject to external economic forces and fluctuating markets. A small business feels the impact of these forces immediately and sometimes lacks the material resources to comfortably weather hard financial times.

Most entrepreneurs are very motivated people. Can you keep going when your motivation is tested by financial challenges, long hours and extended fiscal periods with little or no rewards?

With discipline, yes.

Discipline is refusing to accept *Failure* as an option. It will be your self-discipline that will get you through the tough times. With discipline you know that you'll ultimately succeed, even when others are taking odds against you.

Discipline is the development of habits that move you toward your goals. When times are tough, don't fall into the habit of commiserating with other people who are also miserable. You don't need *sympathy,* you need *energy!* When you feel discouraged, make it your habit to associate with people who are prospering.

When you encounter a failure, make it a habit to learn from your failure. When times are slow, make it a habit to spend time learning new skills and techniques. Every disaster is an opportunity to the disciplined person.

When you succeed, make it your habit to appreciate your success. Make it your habit to recognize those who helped you create your success, and make it a habit to repeat whatever it is you did that got you to your goal.

Successful people repeat successful patterns.

To develop discipline, find something you like to do, and do it! Start with something small. Enjoy every small success, and then move on to greater tasks and goals.

A wonderful opportunity for training discipline is the study of music. Anyone can start learning a musical instrument for a very small investment in time and money.

The great thing about playing music is that it also nourishes your spiritual resources. Learning music is one of the best exercises for the mind. Playing music is both relaxing and energizing at the same time. They say that music soothes the savage beast; this is especially evident when you pick up your guitar or sit at the piano after a hard day at work or school. Music helps reduce stress on the body, expands the mind, and feeds the soul.

You can purchase a starter guitar or keyboard for less than $100. You can take lessons, or simply start with a "teach yourself" video or book. You may be very surprised at how just a little effort every day will produce remarkable results.

When I really need a pick-me-up, there's no better therapy than playing my banjo. Have you ever seen an angry or stressed banjo player?

Most of all, discipline is the habit of constant, mindful and attentive practice. Pick something…and do it every day. You'll enjoy the good feeling that comes from constant self-improvement. Keep at it and you'll eventually know the peace of mind that comes with mastery. This feeling of self-worth is self-propagating and portable. Take this feeling with you into other areas of your life.

Some years ago I attended a seminar with Master Yamazaki. Master Yamazaki is one of the world's most renowned experts in Japanese swordsmanship. As you might imagine, the Japanese take this art very seriously! You might think that Master Yamazaki would be an ultra-serious and stone faced throwback to the legendary ancient Samurai.

I found Master Yamazaki to be an engaging teacher with a great sense of humor. He told a story of a young swordsman who asked his teacher how he too could become a great sword master.

The teacher said the key to mastery is very simple. All you need to do is follow three simple rules:

Rule number one: basic practice.
Rule number two: basic practice.
Rule number three? More basic practice!

Master Yamazaki punctuated his story with this advice in a thick Japanese accent, ***"Like Nike, 'Just Do It!'"***

Through discipline you apply your energy constantly, with unwavering effort toward your goals, and toward your personal vision of success.

For those willing to develop and practice self-discipline, it is the key to freedom.

Time

The third component of the *Kung Fu Triangle* is ***Time.***

As you know from experience, if not from physics, time really is relative. Time is dependent on the perspective of the observer. Broaden your perspective and you increase your capacity to utilize time. If you can accept that it takes time to make substantive changes in your life, you will find more time in which to make those changes.

In contemporary culture, it's common to expect nearly everything right now. If you live in America, you can place an order by phone or on the internet for nearly anything you want, and have it delivered to your door the next day.

Developing self-motivation and discipline takes *time.* Developing personal power takes *time.* You can change the direction of your life in an instant simply by making the decision to improve. To be successful, you've got to sustain your motivation and discipline, and consistently improve yourself, *over time.*

Apply yourself diligently and you can integrate a great deal of knowledge very quickly; you may even develop certain skills quickly, but to fully integrate the true meaning of *Kung Fu* you've got to appreciate the value of sustaining the process of self-improvement over time. The true spirit of *Kung Fu* is the application of motivation and discipline over time.

I recently saw a commercial for the NFL network that really nails the true meaning of *Kung Fu.* The narrator of the commercial delivers this line:

"Amateurs practice until they get it right; professionals practice until they can't get it wrong!"

That's exactly the idea behind *mastery* in martial arts. That's the essence of *Kung Fu.*

Earlier we touched on the ultimate secret of the martial arts, one word: ***practice.*** A goal provides the motivation to practice, however, while actually practicing, the importance of the goal is second to the moment of practice. It's most important to be mindful and to focus on what you're doing right here, and right now. Your ultimate goal is always on the horizon, *but right now you're right where you should be: enjoy being here and now.* Work within this mindset and you'll constantly move toward your goals. Your ultimate goals are made up of the smaller successes you create by focusing and enjoying what you're doing right now; *be in the moment.*

Practicing for the shear joy of it transforms the experience of time to cyclical rather than linear. There will be good days followed by bad, followed again by good. You'll have successes, failures and more successes. Enjoy your time right now and enjoy your practice; and by the way, everything you do is practice!

The only *time* you can change you future is now. When you're fully engaged in practice, here and now, your dreams are becoming realities. The present moment is with you always. You might say the only thing that lasts forever is the present moment.

You can't go back in time to change mistakes; you can only learn and make adjustments here and now. You can't jump ahead in time to claim your prize; you can only participate in the process of making your dreams come true *right now.* You've got to have faith your actions, what you do *now* creates the results you desire in the *future.* This is why it's so important to develop personal power and self-belief. Your success is a direct product of your self-belief and your ability to call on this belief to sustain your efforts *now,* knowing that your reward might not come until *later.*

The trick is to keep this process going over whatever period of time is necessary. This is how time relates back again to discipline. A good working definition of discipline might be: ***"the self-directed habit of producing a sustained effort toward your goals over time."***

So, how much time will it take to reach your goals? Good question; the answer depends on *your* schedule!

It is important to set a time frame for accomplishing any particular goal. Deadlines keep you from procrastinating.

Despite all my metaphysical rambling about time being relative, the fact is that people manage time based on quantifiable increments called minutes, hours, days and years.

Tracking your time keeps you accountable to your personal vision of success. People tend to use time more efficiently when schedules are kept, deadlines are respected, and use of time is analyzed. Frankly, if you don't keep track of your time you can literally lose it. Tracking your time keeps you focused, and helps you appreciate where you are now, relative to where you're going. Time tracking shows you how much closer you are to your goals and how much more time it will take you to reach success.

This, however, isn't a book on time management. My time management bible is Stephen R. Covey's *First Things First.* My job here is to discuss *personal power.* Once you know how to develop and apply personal power, you can use this power to design and achieve your goals. The development of personal power takes some time and you'll need to schedule time for that work. However, the process of developing personal power transcends quantifiable linear time.

How much time does it take to develop personal power? Now that's a GREAT question!

Answer: Forever!

Constantly develop your personal power. Apply the components from each of the *Triangles.* The shape of the triangle implies that each component side supports the others. When *motivation* wanes, apply *discipline.* Apply consistent discipline *over time* and you achieve. Each achievement in turn generates renewed motivation and the cycle continues.

Treat every day, every moment, and every adventure as a new beginning. This is another application of *Beginner's Mind.* No matter how accomplished you become, there's always room for improvement. Rather than spending your time patting yourself on the back with each achievement, enjoy the moment, and then seek out your next adventure.

You could say that no matter how good you get, you can always get better. That's true, but there's a deeper, more practical application for *Beginner's Mind.*

Truly successful people are never satisfied. They may be very *happy*, but never *satisfied.* Keep *Beginner's Mind* and you'll approach each new day and every new opportunity with an open mind and heart. Go ahead and give yourself a quick pat on the back, then look toward how much more *can still be done.*

I've met a few truly great people in my life. I've met many more who *think* they're great. Those who think or even know they're great spend a lot of time patting themselves on the back. Quite a few of them were very happy to tell me how great they were. These people knew everything; had been everywhere and had done everything. They're also usually the people who appear very satisfied with themselves, but seldom seem truly happy. They spend a lot of time complaining and while they always know the answer to all of *my* problems, they can't seem to solve any of their own.

The few truly great people I've met are always trying to learn something new. These people visit the same places a hundred times, and yet have a new experience with each visit. These people find joy in hardship and opportunity in disaster. For these rare people, every achievement establishes a new standard and a new goal; every ending is a new beginning.

Beginner's mind teaches me to start every day asking: "what can I learn today?"

The process of self-improvement is never finished. Perfection is not a destination; it's a never ending process. Full application of the component of *time* requires accepting that you're always a work in progress. Time isn't a specific mark on the clock, and a moment is not necessarily a minute. Time is that experience of life that is with you always. A moment can last forever; a moment well spent can be taken with you and becomes part of every future present moment.

Training in martial arts takes time. It doesn't matter how good we are, we'll still always take the time to improve.

Developing personal power and developing your *self* takes time too. As long as you're alive you've got time to improve. Some people change their lives in the time it takes to draw their final breath. How much time do you really have to develop your *self? I'd say take all the time you need.*

Today we live in the age of instant gratification. We're addicted to instant gratification. One symptom of this addiction is our obsession with fast food. In fact, the secret of the success of the fast food industry is in catering to our *need for speed* when it comes to stuffing our faces as fast as we can as we rush through our busy days. The problem is that most fast food is high in calories and low in nutritional value.

It takes time to prepare a healthful meal. It takes time to care for one's mind, body and spirit. Most truly worthwhile endeavors take time.

That's the way martial arts training works and that's the way self-improvement works. One of my favorite teachers, Dr. Yang Jwing-Ming has a great saying about people starting martial arts training today. "Everybody wants to be a Jedi Knight in two weeks," he says, *"Takes longer than two weeks!"*

Developing personal power takes time. You may experience discouragement, frustration or even hunger along the way. Quality always takes time. Lasting rewards are those paid for with time. If you do experience some frustration along the way, keep remembering that *frustration is the well from which all wisdom springs.*

Over time you come to understand the importance of *taking* your time. You also come to understand the importance of using your time wisely. There's no way to replace a lost moment. Each moment of your life is a precious jewel that must be cherished and appreciated.

You need power to reach your full potential. Personal power is developed through motivation and discipline, over time.

That's "Kung Fu"!

The Energy Triangle

We've been talking about how to develop power, and how power is best applied to produce results. Where does all this power come from? Power doesn't just happen; you need to put something in to get power out. The ***Energy Triangle*** represents the *input* side of the equation.

Powering your life requires an enormous quantity of energy. The sources of human energy are found in the components of the ***Energy Triangle:*** *Body, Mind and Spirit.* Remember, however, that power is not how much energy you put in; power is the quantity of the *result* of your efforts. *Don't confuse power with exertion.*

Body, mind and *spirit* are sources and reservoirs for human energy. If you're the power plant, the water driving your turbines is stored in the reservoirs of your body, mind and spirit.

To power your success you're going to have to be the conservator of these reservoirs. You've got to practice protect, develop and manage these resources to assure an abundant supply of energy. You've got to take care of yourself in three major areas represented by the *Components* of the ***Energy Triangle:***

- ✍ **Body**
- ✍ **Mind**
- ✍ **and Spirit**

These components contain the *energetic resources* you need to develop power.

The connection between body, mind and spirit is *feeling.* Cultivate these energetic reserves and you'll generate positive feelings. As you build your reserves, you increase your feelings of self-confidence, abundance, self-worth and courage,

When you're doing something that feels wrong, you're depleting your reserves. It's obvious! When you constantly drain your reserves without recharging them, you experience guilt, sadness, self-pity, worthlessness, shame, fear and poverty.

The *Energy Triangle* is based on the Chinese concept of "San Qi" *(pronounced "Sahn Chee"). San Qi* literally means "three marvels" and describes the essential components necessary for human life. These components are also called *San Bao,* or *Three Treasures.* Nature provides these treasures; you're the caretaker. Guard and cultivate these treasures and you create a healthy and happy life. The *Treasures* are: *Essence, Energy* and *Spirit.*

In Chinese philosophy *essence,* or *jing,* is the body as it comes fully equipped by nature. You are born with the stuff you need to exist. You might say this is the material or physical manifestation of human existence, however, this can't be separated from the energetic processes that drive the force we call life.

Energy, or *chi,* is life force. *Chi* is whatever it is that permeates every living thing and causes it to be alive. The mind and its processes, including human feelings and emotions, are known as *spirit.*

In the West we tend to recognize a slight semantic difference between *mind* and *spirit. Mind* gives a name to our ability to direct and process the experience of human life. *Spirit* describes whatever it is that makes us human beyond our physical qualities.

The *Energy Triangle* simply translates these ideas to a Western frame of reference. Energy is the universal component; matter is just the momentary perception of a probable energetic event. Now *that's* spooky!

In order to produce power in your life, and particularly if you want to measure power by the production of tangible results including, but not limited to wealth, you've got to take care of your energy resources. You need a fully charged battery to start your car. You need a fully charged body, mind and spirit to start your success.

Is this stuff Real?

We tend to define reality in terms of the stuff you can see, and stuff you can't see. However, if *seeing* is really *believing,* we're in a lot of trouble!

Most of the modern world runs on electricity. We've harnessed and directed the energy of the electron…but nobody has ever seen one, *electron that is.* An atomic blast can level a city, these days several cities at once, but nobody has ever seen an atom.

The proof of the existence of electrons, atoms and other quantum particles is based largely on the effects these theoretical particles produce. The entire study of quantum physics is based on theories deduced from the shadows and trails of ghosts.

Don't we really perceive life the same way?

You know you exist, but *how* do you know? You have feelings, you have a feeling of knowing, but where do these feelings come from? Are you the producer, the director, or the star in the movie of your life? You seem to be all three!

There's no more proof that the mind exists than there is proof that an electron exists. Science provides a neat out clause for this lack of proof; it's called "The Principle of Uncertainty." One example is that you just can't measure the exact position and velocity of an electron at the exact same time. The problem is that the act of observing the position of the electron changes its velocity and vice versa. That's a neat way of saying that what we call an electron is more or less a symbol for its own probable appearance, at a particular moment in time, at a particular point in space. Such is the world of particle physics.

The *mind* is best described for our purposes as a process rather than a physical entity. We know the human mind exists because of our apparent ability to be the observer and the object of observation at the same time. The brain is physical organ. It's the processor in our biological computer, capable of generating actions based on pre-programmed commands.

As far as we know, a computer doesn't know itself; *a person does.* To make matters even more interesting, it seems the human mind can't know itself without changing what it knows.

The Chinese describes this paradox in human terms as the qualities of *substantial* and *insubstantial,* two of the many phenomenon represented by *Yin* and *Yang. Tangible* and *intangible* may sound better to an American ear. There's stuff we can touch, taste, hear and smell, and stuff we can't. There's stuff we can understand, and stuff beyond our understanding; both are part of what any individual human being would define as reality.

Up to now we've been talking about components that can be readily measured and quantified. Psychologists can even measure motivation on a relative scale at any given time. How do you measure the potential energy of the body, mind and spirit? You don't really need to.

Feelings connect the tangible and intangible. *Feeling* is a process of body, mind and spirit. Body, mind and spirit are not really separate entities. They're simply the best descriptions we have for different aspects of the life experience. We'd choke on the concept of life as a whole. We need to digest life in spoonfuls, one sting of our senses, one spark of creative thought, and one brilliant flash of insight at a time.

I've got to be brutally honest with you. This is the most difficult area to for me to talk about. You can't directly measure power in body, mind and spirit. Here I'm talking relatively, about how you *feel,* more than what you can actually do. I'm talking about how to cultivate a feeling of health and wealth in body, mind and spirit to create the energy you need to develop personal power. Feelings are completely subjective, yet our subjectivity is influenced by objective conditions, environment and culture.

What I am really talking about is how much you believe in yourself, and in your capacity to achieve your goals. You can't believe in yourself when you're feeling deficient or impoverished in mind, body and spirit.

If you want to achieve, you've got to believe.

I've already stated that I don't believe that positive thinking, or belief, is all you need to produce success. You need to take action. So what does all this "quantum soup" stuff have to do with producing real success and happiness?

All action requires power. You need to cultivate and access these sources of human energy to develop power. You can measure the potential energy stored in a battery with a volt meter; you measure your human energy resources through feelings.

You're going to rely on feeling to help you build your personal power reserves. You're going to trust these feelings because they're more real to you than any supposedly tangible bits and pieces sticking in your consciousness at any given time.

Let's call these supposedly tangible bits *memories.* Whatever we think and do from this moment on is somewhat dependent on what we've experienced and how we process and store experiences as memory. How you process whatever you're experiencing in the present moment is in large part dependent on your memory. Your current perception of events is relative to what you've fixed in your memory from past experiences and how you now perceive these bits in the context of your present frame of reference.

Once you've touched a hot stove, you don't need to touch it again to know it's hot. You've processed this experience and recorded it as a memory. Next time you see a burner you draw upon this memory and make a conscious decision as to whether or not you should touch the stove.

This process of experience, memory and reflection is the process of *feeling.* Sometimes we're dealing with simple feelings of pure physical pain or pleasure. Sometimes we work with the more complex feelings associated with emotions.

Feelings and emotions are part of the human experience. Feelings and emotions happen largely as a result of exposure to certain stimuli, and the brain's biological response to stimuli, predicated on trained and instinctive memory.

Feelings and emotions may, to a degree, be products of the biological processes you've inherited from nature. Your *response* to feelings and emotions is up to you, subject to your own life experience. Some of that experience comes from the culture into which you happened to be born, and home environment in which you were raised.

You can't change where you were born and how you were raised; from this moment on you can make some choices. As soon as you process and assimilate new information and experiences, you can begin the conscious process of deciding how you're going to react to what you now know and feel.

Feelings can help you create who you are now, and help you move beyond who you used to be. Feelings recalled from memory are imprints off what you were. Feelings you create and nourish today are the blueprints for who you want to become in the future.

Today, you may feel successful, or you might feel like a failure. Are those feelings a result of who you are today, or are those feelings a product of past actions and circumstances? Here you find one of the most significant intersections of thought and realization.

What you're feeling today shapes who you will be tomorrow. Feelings of self-doubt, poverty, self-deprecation and failure are likely to manifest failure today, and in the future. If you want to create future success, you've got to start cultivating feelings that support self-confidence, positive thought, positive action and success...*today.*

You create who you are. Your feelings are a reflection of your past, a snapshot of your present and a projection of your future.

Feelings are not material entities; feelings are an energetic process of human life. Direct your feelings and you control the production of human energy in your life. You become the director, as well as the star, in the movie of your life.

Body

Body is at first glance the easiest energetic component to understand. The body defines physicality. What we call the physical world is largely dependent on how we interact with the universe through the processes of the body. It's our direct connection to the rest of the universe. You can see your body, weigh your body, touch it, and touch other human bodies.

Your body is the most tangible source and manifestation of human energy. Your body is, in fact, mostly energy, lots of it! A 150 pound human being has the potential atomic energy of over 60 Hiroshima bombs.[18] It's a good thing you're fairly stable from an atomic perspective!

It's also kind of sad that with all this energy at our disposal, some people can't access enough energy to get off the couch.

Human beings generally experience the phenomenon of *mind* as at least renting space in the anatomical organ of the body called the brain. The mind and body are inseparable aspects of the singular experience of human existence.

You need a lot of energy to keep your brain operating properly. In fact, the human brain consumes nearly twelve times the amount of energy of the rest of the body. If the mind is at least metaphorically a tenant of the brain, you need a healthy, energetic body to keep the lights on.

Another ancient Chinese wise-guy named Wen Tzu put it this way…

"The body is the temple of life. Energy is the force of life. Spirit is the governor of life. If one of them goes off balance, all three are damaged."[19]

The mind controls the body, but the mind as we know it can't exist without the body. Nurture the body and you also nurture the mind.

A researcher named Jean Pierre Changeux, at the famous Pasteur Institute, quantified that simple muscle movement stimulates the growth of axons that communicate signals between neurons. The more axons you have, the more intelligent you tend to be. A team at the University of California found that children exercising an hour a day are more intelligent than those who don't. Many researchers have duplicated these findings.[20] This research confirms that conditioning the body improves the mind.

Fact: Football players are far more intelligent than Couch Potatoes!

If you doubt this fact, start a journal. Record how you feel when you dedicate some time to personal exercise. Compare this to how you feel when you're too busy to get to the gym.

Failure to care for the body causes stress. Stress is costing the American economy over 300 billion dollars a year![21] To this cost, add the additional expenses of health care, insurance, and non-insured medical treatment for people who are sick because of life-style choices like smoking, drug and alcohol abuse, and unhealthy eating habits.

It's very easy to make excuses and avoid taking care of your body. I've become a bit more hard-core with my advice to others in this area. A few years ago I sat with a father of one of my martial arts students. He told me that his doctor gave him about six months to change his life or his prognosis was for serious heart trouble, perhaps even open heart surgery.

In past years I would have listened compassionately- and helped this person commit suicide, *compassionately.* His primary excuse for his lack of exercise was that it would take too much time away from his kids.

BANG! I asked, "How much time are you going to have to spend with your family, *when you're dead?"* Now that's a compassionate question! I said, "Your son is practicing martial arts, why don't you join too?" A couple of years later this guy earned his black belt, as did his son. He lost weight, toned his body and improved the course of his life dramatically. Best of all, he increased the time he has to share with his children.

Asian philosophers draw no hard line between mind and body. Mind and body, as separate entities, is an illusion; simply a product of the way we perceive our human life through our limited perceptions.

To access the potential power of a healthy and active mind; take time to nourish a healthy and active body.

Mind

The *mind* is not the *brain* any more than a person is just a body. A person is the sum of the thoughts, ideas, desires, ambitions and actions expressed through the movements and processes of the body over a period we call a lifetime; the body is the vehicle for this expression. The mind is the source of our feelings, emotions, perceptions, thoughts and ideas; the brain is the organ of the body that seems to house the physiological mechanics associated with the phenomenon we experience as the mind. A body is not itself a person; and a brain is not itself, a mind.

You may be physically attracted to a set of identical twins, yet only have feelings of falling in love with one. What's the difference? These two people might look alike, and even act in just about the same way, yet you might have completely different *feelings* for one over the other. If the body were the person, either twin would inspire identical feelings of love. If the brain were the mind, you wouldn't care which.

In Chinese philosophy, this process of the discriminating mind is called *Taiji (Also "Tai Chi").*

Some might describe the mind as simply a *process* of the brain. Philosophically we run into some problems here as well. The brain is a physical organ, part of the body, and doesn't exist outside itself. The mind can go wherever you want it to and isn't limited to the confines of the body. The mind can even contemplate its own existence!

So, is the mind just the end result of a series of random biochemical and bioelectrical processes associated with the brain? Or, does our human intuition tell us that the mind is something more?

The Quantum Philosopher-Scientist, Dr. Fred Alan Wolf, offers this interesting perspective:

"I am a body. At least that is how I scientifically think about my physical self-as an entity, a substantial being, a living physical object. But I also have feelings, thoughts, and sensations which tell me that I am not just a body. And, I intuit that at some deep level, beyond what I can see or feel, I am not just my feelings, thoughts, and sensations either. My intuition tells me that I am more than my body; more, even, than my feelings, thoughts and sensations."[22]

It's hard to believe that a human life is an accidental birth, bursting from the womb of some cosmic chemical spill. The very fact that the human mind experiences awareness of itself somehow causes us to feel that we're something more than a series of electrochemical processes, ignited by some random primordial spark.

I once had an interesting conversation with a physician who was explaining the electrochemical processes of the brain. I was fascinated as he very succinctly reduced nearly every human activity to a series of these processes. *(Am I a geek, or what?)*

At any rate, I was soon to become a big pain in the ass to the doctor, who obviously knew a great deal more about these things than I did. Every time he eloquently described how certain chemicals initiated the release of hormones and caused this and that to occur I simply asked him, "OK…where'd *that* come from?"

As he painted his detailed picture of the intricate biomechanics underlying human thoughts and actions, I just kept asking him, "Where'd *that* come from?" Eventually we reached a stalemate. I wasn't trying to discredit him; in fact I learned a great deal, and was very appreciative that he shared his time and knowledge with me. His theory, that every action in my life was simply the random firing of predictable biochemical reactions, just didn't feel *complete.*

This very knowledgeable doctor couldn't tell me where an idea comes from; he could only tell me what happens once the idea is already present.

I fired my last desperate shot. I asked him to reach down and tie his shoe. As he did I asked, "Where'd *that* come from?" He started to reply, "I *decided…*" Point, game, match!

Well, not quite. I don't know where ideas come from either; but come they do!

According to some studies the human mind is capable of producing 36,000 thoughts per hour. That's about 10 thoughts per waking second![23] No wonder we're so confused so much of the time!

If you approach the issue from an evolutionary standpoint, you might say that human thought is a conditioned response to stimuli, programmed by generations of human development. You could also approach the issue from a religious standpoint and say that thought, or at least the capacity for thought, is a gift from God.

OK, in either case, where'd that come from?

No matter which perspective, the one mystery that remains is that human beings appear to have free-will. In other words, it doesn't matter whether the human mind is a result of winning the great cosmic lottery, or a divine gift granted by a creative and superior being. As a human being, it still seems to me that I'm able to make up my own mind, once I realize I have one. It's a wonderful quality of human life that you apparently can and do make up your own mind. It seems that most of the time, anyway, you can choose what you're going to do and how you're going to do it.

Don't confuse my philosophy with a casual *if-it-feels-good-do-it* attitude. Free-will comes with great responsibility: Every time you make a decision, set a goal, and initiate action, you can and do impact the lives of others.

In order to live in harmony with fellow human beings and the other citizens of nature, it's important that you follow some rules. These rules should encourage the creativity and productivity of the individual while assuring that each individual is protected, as much as possible, from harm caused by the poor decisions of others.

To me it's very simple. If your thoughts and actions are positive and contribute to human development, you're probably doing the right thing. When your thoughts and actions cause harm without justification, you're probably doing wrong. Of course the element of *justification* leaves open a lot of grey areas, and many people are not predisposed to committing a lot *grey matter* when it comes to reconciling these grey areas.

As you cultivate the energy and power of the mind, it's essential to accept this truth: *your thoughts and actions impact others.*

Observe the "Rule of Respect." Generate thoughts and actions based on caring for self and one-another. Mistakes will sometimes be made, but cultivating a respectful mind turns mistakes into lessons, mitigates damage, and makes any mistake part of a future success. A person with a respectful energetic mind accepts personal responsibility, learns from mistakes, and moves forward in a positive direction.

One of the most influential instructors in modern martial arts is Grandmaster Jhoon Rhee. Master Rhee founded one of the largest and most dynamic martial arts organizations in the world. His "retirement" is dedicated to sharing his philosophy with other martial artists, and encouraging us to develop our power and resources in order to better our communities.

I attended one of Master Rhee's lectures in which he shared a powerful set of personal affirmations. One of them was:

"I never make mistakes…KNOWINGLY."

As human beings, we're inevitably going to make mistakes. What's important is to learn from them. It's our responsibility to ourselves and others not to commit an act when we are *knowingly* aware of its negative impact on others.

Another of Master Rhee's affirmations is:

"I am happy because I choose to be happy!"

Personal responsibility comes from a fundamental acceptance of the human capacity to act with free-will. If every action is predetermined, how can I possibly be held accountable for any action, positive or negative?

My entire belief in the ability to develop, cultivate and express personal power stands on this principle:

I am the only person responsible for my personal success and happiness. Success and happiness are the products of a healthy mind, inseparable from the body. I must take care of the mind, body and spirit in order to develop and express power for my benefit, and the benefit of others.

It's up to me to cultivate my mind, and just like the body, the mind needs exercise. I use two *personal* techniques for training the mind and two *community* techniques.

My first personal technique is meditation. You may have a different word or different specific techniques. You may call it *prayer,* although there can be a subtle semantic distinction between *prayer* and *meditation.* Prayer may be meditative and reflective; however, meditation can be practiced without the communal relationship to a higher being generally associated with prayer. Whatever you want to call it, to cultivate the mind you need to practice deliberate and mindful contemplation. You need to spend some time in a restorative and peaceful state.

I use a simple combination of meditation exercises each morning. My wake-up routine is divided into three sections:

I start with a simple set of *Qigong (pronounced "Chee Gong")* exercises. These exercises are designed to stimulate circulation in the body and energize the mind to start the day. You might substitute a morning stretch, a walk, or some other gently stimulating exercise. I teach some of my favorite *Qigong* sets on a video titled ***The Energy Tapes: Basic Qigong,*** available on *www.JimBouchard.org.*

Next I spend a minimum of 5 minutes just sitting and breathing. My practice sometimes includes specific exercises to cultivate internal energy, but generally this segment of my meditation consists of simply sitting quietly and *being.* I'm not trying to accomplish anything in particular; I'm simply taking time to recharge my human energy battery by doing what is most natural and basic to human life: *breathing.*

The final section, again a minimum of 5 minutes, is for *Directed Meditation.* I'm directing my thoughts toward what I want to accomplish in the future, and for the rest of the day. This is when I'll focus on specific goals. This exercise helps me start my day with a positive and confident mindset.

After my directed meditation period, I finish with my next personal mind exercise: *learning.* I choose a book or an article important to my current goals and activities and spend a minimum of a half-hour reading and studying. I usually try to devote at least an hour, but I've set the half-hour minimum to make sure I won't make an excuse to skip this vital exercise before I attack the rest of my schedule.

Napoleon Hill, one of the pioneers in modern self-improvement training, said your success over the course of a year is dependent upon "the books you read and the people you meet." What more productive way to start the day than by reading some material specific to achieving your goals?

My first *community technique* for conditioning the mind is a natural extension of the personal technique of learning: it is *teaching*. Effective teaching springs from sincere learning. The stream of learning is deepened through teaching. For some years, I've learned more by teaching martial arts than I have from my own practice. Some of my most powerful lessons come from my students, particularly beginning students, and some of them are only 4 years old!

Some years ago I visited a local elementary school to talk about respect. I always start this presentation the same way; I ask a simple question, "Does anyone know the meaning of the word 'respect?'"

On this particular day a first grade student raised his hand, stood up, and said…

"Sensei, respect means taking care of one another."

Have you ever heard a better definition? I bowed to this brilliant young man, and from that moment adopted his definition as my own. He was the teacher that day; I was the student.

Being a constant student is one of the best ways to train and condition the mind. By organizing and sharing your thoughts through teaching, you'll forge tools you can use to further craft your mind and develop mastery. Learning from your students is yet another expression of *Beginner's Mind. Beginner's Mind* reminds us of the power of constant, life-long learning.

Modern medical science is now substantiating the importance of learning as an ongoing and necessary part of our health and well-being. The paradigm has shifted from "aging lowers ability," to: "use it or lose it!"[24] Engaging in mentally stimulating activities improves health and may help prevent diseases like Alzheimer's.

Through my study I've found another powerful *community* exercise for training the mind: *Communication!*

Almost any human interaction stimulates thinking and improves the mind. Games, sports, conversation, debate, learning and teaching all contribute to a healthy and powerful mind. That's why it's so important to take off the headphones, walk away from the TV, and simply spend some time really communicating with one another! Paying attention to one another also cultivates feelings of worth and acceptance and induces a positive attitude.

Study, contemplate, reflect, communicate; these are the gymnastics of the mind. Don't just think about art, create some! Do you like listening to music? Play some! Learn a new language; learn how to cook or fix your car. Almost any creative and thoughtful activity will do.

Combine physical and mindful exercise and you'll multiply the results! This is where athletes get their *edge.* Play games; participate in sports, *practice martial arts! (I had to slip that one in!)*

Chinese philosophy recognizes two distinct personalities of the mind. *Monkey Mind* is the emotional mind, always jumping around chasing bananas. The *Monkey Mind* is creative and spirited. The *Monkey Mind* can also be obsessive.

There's an old Asian folktale about how to trap a monkey. You'll need a jar with an opening just large enough to drop in a peach. Tie the jar to a tree or a stake. Put the jar near a monkey. Wait.

Eventually, the monkey will reach into the jar to get the peach. His problem is that the opening of the jar isn't big enough to get his hand out, as long as he's holding on to the peach! If he's stuck in *Monkey Mind* mode, and being a monkey, that's quite likely; you've captured yourself a monkey!

Have you ever felt trapped like the monkey?

We've got to learn when to let go.

Horse Mind is the cultivated, intellectual mind. Use *Horse Mind* to control and direct your life the same way the rider controls the horse. The animal supplies the *horse power;* the rider *directs* this power to get where he wants to go.

If our monkey had accessed his horse mind, he would have thought rationally about his situation. He might have delayed his desire for gratification and let go of the peach in order to escape the trap.

Both *minds* are important. The monkey is creative, playful and energetic. The horse is powerful, focused and productive.

Let the Monkey Mind out to play from time to time; just be sure the Horse Mind is in charge!

Spirit

Spirit is the spark of life; the unseen, unheard voice of the conscience, the instinctive drive to live.

Spirit is courage.

Spirit is the source of all human energy imbued by nature both within and beyond the scope of body and mind.

We can't weigh *spirit.* We can't measure its length or width. We can't really see it; we can only see its reflection in actions and memories.

We *can* feel spirit. We can touch it, internally, through feelings; and through our feelings we're in touch *with* it. We know spirit exists mostly because we know, somehow, that we can't exist without it.

Defining spirit is nearly impossible in any way that transcends cultural or even individual understanding. Still, libraries are full of endless volumes of writing on the spirit. Any definition of *spirit* starts and ends with an attempt to define that which cannot be defined. You know spirit is real only through your experience, and no other way.

The Chinese put it this way:

"The Tao that's named is no longer the Tao."

Science is constantly looking for the "Unified Theory" that reconciles the processes of the universe. Since *The Tao* is literally translated as *The Way,* maybe *Tao* isn't such a bad word for *however it is the universe operates.* At any rate, scientists and philosophers both face the same problem: no matter how clearly we define the operations of nature, there always seems to be exceptions to the rules. To most of us this simply means the *grand ultimate* operation of the universe is way over our heads!

But even so, we humans with our limited perceptions and capacity for understanding want to know a little bit about how we fit into this grand scheme. We seem to be born with an inherent desire to at least attempt to understand who we are and why we're here.

We might not be able to fully understand nature as a whole, or our part in it, but we've got to start someplace! That's why we break these grand concepts into smaller, more digestible bits.

For us to wrestle with the grandest of all questions, who and what we are, we *do* need some labels. Given our limited perceptions and understanding, we've got to work with smaller concepts and ideas we can name and talk about.

Let's use the label *Spirit* for that part of ourselves we can feel, but can't weigh, for that part of us that extends beyond the boundaries of the body, for that part of us that reaches into the future, for that part of us that allows us to direct and create our future through the power of ideas.

The word *spirit* is often misunderstood and misused. I'm not using the words *spirit* and *spiritual* in a religious context. I'm talking about the conditions and qualities of the human experience that are difficult, if not impossible, to measure and quantify.

As a resource, spirit is that part of human life that transcends intellectual understanding, can't be proven, but is sorely missed when it's not there. I'm referring to whatever it is that precedes human life, but makes human life possible; the encoded spark of desire for us to live and prosper.

Spirit and soul might be the same thing; I don't know. I don't pretend to be a theologian any more than I pretend to be a physicist. I'm just trying to direct the course of my life using the knowledge and wisdom available within and around me.

Semantically, spirit also refers to courage. Courage is the capacity to act in the face of fear, danger or risk.

Some people confuse courage with an absence of fear. Please don't make that mistake. The absence of fear isn't courage; ***the absence of fear is stupidity!*** You can manage fear through preparation, training, and rational assessment of risks. Thoughtless action in the face of real danger is simply stupid, not brave.

You need *courage* to be a positive person. It takes courage and discipline to expect success even in the face of failure. You face obstacles and challenges every day; you need courage to maintain a positive attitude and to find the great opportunities that exist in every failure or adversity.

Study people who have made the greatest contributions to humanity and you'll find a nearly universal theme: nearly all remarkably great achievements emerge from tremendous adversity. Some people seem to use adversity as fertilizer for growing success. With courage, they can see beyond any current challenges. To successful people:

"Every disaster is an opportunity."

The most dangerous enemy of success is not failure, it is negativity. Too many people throw in the towel just before their moment of victory. You don't remember the fighter who dodged all worthy challengers; the most memorable fighter is the underdog who faced the champ, fought his way back from the ropes after being rocked to his core, and won against all odds.

You need plenty of spirit and courage to overcome negativity. Contemporary culture reeks of negativity. Try to avoid negativity for just one day; you'll probably have to unplug your TV, radio and internet connection. You may have to stay away from most of the people at work. You might even have to go on a long hike in a secluded wilderness area where your only companions will be moose and bear, and you better hope they haven't read the newspaper that day.

As if it weren't bad enough, there's now a booming entertainment franchise built on exploiting the horrors of real life: *reality television* is becoming a plague. As if life weren't tough enough, producers have found a way to show us the worst side of humanity by amplifying human conflict and dysfunctional behavior, solely for our entertainment.

Some negativity is caused by an understandable natural fear of risk and pain; however, the parents of every great achievement are risk and pain.

Some negativity is the result of healthy skepticism. I am a healthy skeptic. I will not teach that sitting and visualizing a million dollars will produce even your first dollar, no matter how much time you dedicate or how devout your efforts. I do know that even a moment spent visualizing a million dollars, if that's your goal, will get you much closer to your first dollar than spending that same moment visualizing all the probable reasons you *can't* realize your goal.

It is true that there are circumstances beyond your control. Good things do happen to bad people, and bad things sometimes happen to good people.

It's equally true that you can control a great deal about what happens in your life. Allow skepticism, fear and pain to paralyze you and you surrender any positive outcomes purely to chance. If that's how you feel about life, you may as well stay home, collect welfare, and use your welfare payments to buy lottery tickets.

If you want some control over your success, if you want to increase the probability of success, then *The Way* is to embrace the hard work and discipline necessary to develop a positive mind and cultivate spirit.

I've always found it easier to face real physical danger than to face emotional negativity, particularly when this negativity was self-inflicted. Tell your friends about your wildest dreams. How many will say "Go for it!"? Will some tell you it's impossible, stupid or too risky? Factor money into the equation; tell a group of your closest friends you're going to risk your life savings on a new business venture, see who encourages you and who thinks you're nuts.

You've got to develop courage to practice and sustain a positive mental attitude, a positive spiritual state of being and to generate positive results.

The only way to develop courage is to face challenges and achieve victories. Of course, you need courage to face challenges. Don't worry, we're all endowed with some little seed courage and spirit; it's called *the will to live.*

We presume that every human being is endowed with certain inalienable rights; we're definitely endowed with inalienable desires. Among these are the desires for "life, liberty, and the pursuit of happiness."

From your seed of spirit and courage, you'll need to find activities and exercises that expose you to challenges and allow you the opportunity for victory and success. The more you succeed, the more confidence and courage you develop and the stronger your spirit becomes. Challenging exercises don't necessarily have to involve physical dangers; some of us just prefer those that do!

Individual and team sports provide a terrific opportunity to develop courage and spirit. I'm a little biased towards football, but most sports demand some degree of courage while reducing the risk of physical injury. Golf announcers use the word *courage* when describing the ability of the champion to maintain focus and battle back from a tough round.

Many of the people I admire developed their sense of courage and spirit through military service. If that's not your style, civic service including local politics, volunteer firefighting, and emergency medicine, can provide challenging training ground for developing courage and spirit.

The trick is to find something challenging and face the challenge. Most people fear public speaking; join Toastmasters! If you think you've got some talent in the arts, create some art and share it with the public: write, sing, dance, act; do something outside your comfort zone and you expand your courage and spirit. Express yourself; take a chance by sharing your expression with others. How you do that is completely up to you.

The broader term for phenomenon relating to the spirit is *spiritual.* The word *spiritual* refers to feelings and phenomenon that are beyond understanding from the perspective of physics. You might substitute the word *metaphysical,* but to my ear *spiritual* has a nicer ring.

Scientists now know a great deal about the processes of human thought. The act of tying your shoe can be charted and graphed as a series of bioelectric and biochemical processes. No matter how detailed the map of the physical processes associated with thinking; there is still very little, if any understanding of the origin of the thought!

Where does the *thought* come from? What is the origin of our will to live? Why do we have the innate desire to live, to be free, to be happy or to be with one another?

There are a lot of people who say that all human emotions and spiritual experiences are simply part of the process of preserving and propagating the species. There are too many exceptions for this hypothesis to hold up.

For everything beyond the rational, you can apply the word *spiritual.* It's not important that we share the same religious or philosophical perspective. It is important that you recognize that you have to cultivate a sense of *spiritual abundance* in order to generate power in your life.

The origin of spiritual feelings is often expressed in literature as residing in the *heart.* Not the heart as a mechanical pump, but the heart as the place where we feel our connection with our spiritual nature and resources.

When you're about to meet someone whose approval is important to you, do you feel tightness in the chest? When you really, really, really desire something, don't we say we feel our desire in the heart? How about when you feel profound love? What about our longing for a connection to God or another spiritual being?

Most people would say that they experience these feelings in the *heart.* That's why poets and sages have always used the heart as the metaphor for feelings of love and longing.

I've learned to trust the feelings of my heart. I've also found the heart is the best guide as to whether my thoughts or actions are right or wrong. I believe a healthy person tends toward goodness and possesses a natural revulsion to evil.

I know this because I feel it: in my heart.

I do believe in objective good and evil. Intellectually, the difference is obvious. If I am acting in a way that promotes positive human development; I'm promoting goodness. If I am acting in a manner destructive to human development or purposely harmful to others; my actions are evil. This explanation of good and evil transcends the parameters of culture, education, relative morality or radical ethnocentricity.

Of course, there is a problem with my explanation. In the real world a person's understanding of good and evil are influenced, if not wholly dependent upon culture, education, morality and ethnocentricity. For those people I can still practice compassion, even when I have to oppose them or treat them as an enemy in order to protect myself and others.

To make matters more complex, there are individuals who enjoy good feelings from committing acts of cruelty, abuse and violence. We usually consider these people *anti-social.* They're the anomaly, not the desired norm.

Assuming that I'm of sound mind, my personal experience teaches me that evil actions cause feelings of scarcity, imbalance, discomfort, guilt, anger, hostility, sadness, jealousy, inadequacy, and loneliness. Positive actions create the feelings of abundance, love, sharing, respect, joy, success, self-worth, happiness, and belonging.

How do I know whether my thoughts or actions are good or evil? ***I may know it in my mind, but I feel it in my heart!***

When I'm teaching adult classes, I generally talk about martial arts in terms of *awareness.* When I'm teaching kids I teach them the two most important words in martial arts: *pay attention.*

Have you ever been in the middle of doing something you just knew in your heart was wrong? Intellectually you might have rationalized the behavior, but what you were doing just didn't *feel right.* Pay attention! These feelings are *real!*

On the other hand, your intellectual mind will sometimes put up a struggle, even when your heart tells you it's time to act. You might consider a bold business move; it may be risky because it's innovative and untried. Your rational mind might be saying "don't do it, you might get hurt!" You may still feel in your heart that it's the right thing to do.

When should you listen to the mind and when should you listen to the heart?

Scholars of the *San Qi* say that the spirit is the governor of life. The spirit transcends rational thought; most great accomplishments also transcend rational thought. The spirit speaks through the heart.

I'm not saying ignore rationality, far from it, just be sure you're not bound by it either. Mindless impulsive action can be irresponsible. Isn't it usually better to do *some* thinking before you act? You've got to consider mindfully how your actions will affect your life, and the lives of others.

However, it can be just as dangerous if you never act from the gut. Sometimes your first impulse is right. Sometimes you can miss a great opportunity if you allow your intellectual mind too much time for over-analysis.

Once again you can call on the fundamental component of *balance.* Develop a sense of when to act boldly and when to stop and consider. Practice awareness and develop a sense of your part in nature, and your role in the lives of others. Connect to that which is bigger than all of us.

In order to act courageously you've got to cultivate that part of yourself that understands that you're part of something bigger. Life is very precious and important; it's also quite impermanent. Your life is part of the lives of many others like you. What you do impacts many other lives, now, and in the future.

In other words, what you do may be as important as who you think you are! Your spirit is what connects you to this reality and the voice of the spirit is the heart.

An old Chinese proverb says "Victory in battle is 10% technique and 90% spirit." To be happy and successful, develop your spirit to be happy and successful. Pay the price: have the courage to develop your *Self.*

Develop your spirit and courage by nourishing the Spiritual areas of life.

What are these areas? What can you do to cultivate power in a spiritual sense?

First and foremost practice right behavior. The Japanese call this practice *kata.* This is the name we use in martial arts for the choreographed sequences of movements we use to train the mind and body.

Spiritual *kata* consists of practicing ethical, positive action. Do you treat others with respect? Do you help those around you? Are you supportive of your community and your environment? You can create spiritual kata by becoming involved in any or all of these areas.

You can cultivate spirit through solo practices and by practicing with others. Solo practices include meditation, prayer, and many forms of creative arts. Community practices involve congregating with other people who share positive goals, objectives or beliefs. These practices include group meditation, continuing education or study, community arts like theater and ensemble music, some sports and of course, martial arts classes!

The practice of religion or other focused spiritual activities can help you develop spiritually both alone and through congregation with others.

Join.

Join any positive group or endeavor. Join a church group. Join a civic organization. Volunteer your time or serve a non-profit group. Teach, coach, become a Den Mother or a Brownie Leader. Join Big Brothers/Big Sisters, visit the elderly or deliver meals to shut-ins.

You cultivate spirit by facing challenges, by spending time nourishing your *self* and by extending yourself to others. The important thing to remember is to maintain balance in your spiritual practices just as you do in the other key areas of your life.

Let's say you find great energy in the practice of solitary meditation, but you also have a family. It's important to maintain a balance between the amount of time you spend in your practice and the time you spend with your family.

Gichin Funakoshi, the father of modern martial arts, said that martial arts are to enhance life, not detract from it. The trick is to balance the time you spend alone with quality family time. You might share a portion of your solo practice by teaching willing family members how to practice as well.

On the other hand, it's also important not to lose yourself in the lives of others. The best possible thing you can do for others is to constantly improve yourself. This is the primary reason I put so much emphasis on personal power. When you nourish your *self* and make yourself powerful you become a much greater resource to those around you. If you don't take care of yourself, you're simply not much use to anyone else.

There are hundreds if not thousands of ways to nourish your spiritual self. Many people find all they need in the practice of a particular religion. Most people find great spiritual energy in creative activities such as art, writing and music. Many of us also enjoy spiritual renewal through any activity that brings us close to nature such as hiking, sailing or camping.

My intention here isn't to list all the many ways you can cultivate mind, body and spirit. I hope I've impressed how important this cultivation is to the development of your personal power and to your achievement of success and happiness. Now, go out and find positive activities that make you feel good and cultivate your spirit.

Pay attention to your feelings. When you find something that truly gives you a feeling of transcendence over the normal hum of daily life, then embrace and engage in that activity. You've got to feed the spirit just as you'd feed the body and the mind!

Cultivate all three components of the *Energy Triangle: body, mind* and *spirit,* and you create energetic wealth to power all your ambitions!

Before I leave this chapter I feel obligated to make one point clear beyond any possibility of misunderstanding. It's not your responsibility to read my mind; it's my responsibility to make my thoughts as clear as I possibly can.

The ***Dynamic Components*** is a philosophy of ***action.*** I *do not believe* that positive thought alone can guarantee positive results. I *do not believe* that positive action is a guarantee of success and happiness.

I *know* that positive thought and action are ***essential*** if you want to produce success and happiness.

I *do not believe* that any of us can move or materialize objects through the energetic power of the thinking mind.

I *know* that every thought is at once an energetic entity and a process that initiates human action which can then produce tangible results. To me there's no greater mystery and miracle in the universe than that of the function and origin of the human mind.

I know I'm alive.

Through this experience of life I am connected with the universe.

I experience this connection in my body.

I process this connection in my mind.

I feel this connection in my spirit.

Success: Putting the Dynamic Components to Work

Student: *Master, I'll miss you.*
Master: *Where are you going?*
Student: *I've completed my studies. It's time for me to go out and see the world.*
Master: *What is your ambition?*
Student: *To teach and help others be happy.*
Master: *After your years of travel, where would you like to be?*
Student: *Like you, I'd like to return to the temple and spend the rest of my life here…teaching.*
Master: *You've not yet taken a single step, yet you're already here!*

We are all created for success. I know this to be true with every fiber of my being. I know this to be true because it *feels* true. I need no other proof. Success feels good. Lack of success feels bad, however…

Only YOU can define your personal success.

Now that you're familiar with the ***Dynamic Components of Personal Power,*** you can use these principles to help you design and realize your own personal vision of success. The *Components* provide direction for creating thoughts and actions that improve the probability of realizing your goals and objectives, and ultimately, to create true success.

Your personal vision of success is what you desire, shaped by what you consider to be possible.

What if you create a vision that for the time being seems impossible? If so, your first step is to reduce what now seems impossible, to something possible. You do this by starting to develop the skills and resources you need to make the possible more probable.

Keep the *Energy Triangle* in mind as you begin the process of defining your personal vision of success. The components of *body, mind & spirit* represent the areas in life that are the sources of all human power. The foundational work of making your success more probable is to increase your personal power resources in the key areas of life diagramed in the Energy Triangle.

When you're actively engaged in the process of self-perfection, you are developing self-belief and confidence. You become more skilled in the areas diagramed by the *Kung Fu Triangle;* this process creates an awareness of new possibilities and greater personal potential.

Your potential is stored in reservoirs of knowledge, health, money and goodwill/fame. What you know, who you know, who you are, and what you have; you draw from these reservoirs to generate your success.

Learning and constant self-perfection nourishes the mind and feeds your emotional and spiritual resources. Embrace new challenges and opportunities to grow emotionally, spiritually and physically, and to increase the potential of your mind, body and spirit. Choose personally enriching activities in all 3 areas.

Keep this important point in mind as you begin the process of developing your personal vision of success:

All success is created first in the mind before it is manifest inside and outside the body.

I often tell my students that the "secret" of the martial arts is *practice.* This is true; however, it's probably more accurate to say that ***mindful positive practice creates success.*** Mindful positive practice works in personal life, and works just as well in business and professional life.

In the *dojo* we mindfully practice the positive outcome of a martial arts technique. In real life we need to mindfully practice the positive outcome of each of our goals and objectives. This practice starts with thought and extends to action.

There may be forces pulling us off course every day. We need to develop discipline in this practice of positive thought and action. I'm not the first to say this and I'm sure I won't be the last. Every teacher I admire, living and long since passed, emphasizes positive thought and action as the basis of all human success.

Don't trust me! Read the words of Jesus, Lao Tzu, Buddha, Confucius, and Mohammed. Read Einstein, Martin Luther King, The Dalai Lama, Thicht Naht Than, Kennedy, Reagan, the choice is yours. Read Jack Canfield, Napoleon Hill, Dale Carnegie, Thomas Stanley and others who have made a scientific study of success.

Study successful people and you'll find the same formulas again and again.

Success is created through positive thoughts and actions, constructed on a foundation of faith.

Some people flinch at mention of the word *faith;* however, you've got to develop faith that your thoughts and actions are going to eventually produce desired results. At the very least you need to have faith in your capacity to acquire the skill and knowledge necessary to succeed. No success is ever achieved without faith.

You need to believe in your in yourself in order to maintain your motivation and discipline over time, particularly in the face of adversity. Faith is your bridge from impossible to possible, from possible to probable, and from probable to actual.

Albert Einstein once said,

"I think and think for months, for years. Ninety-nine times the conclusion is false. The hundredth time I am right"[25]

Einstein had a great deal of faith that his ideas were, somehow, true. This faith kept him going in spite of failure and criticism. You may or may not have Einstein's IQ, but you can be his equal or even better him in personal belief.

I tell all my martial arts students that they can become black belts; this is the truth. I don't know who *will,* but I know they all *can* become black belts. The first step is simply to believe that it's possible.

Once you define what your personal success is going to look and feel like, and you start to believe that success is possible, take action.

Cultivate power through the components of the *Kung Fu Triangle: motivation and discipline over time.* Success requires consistent, dedicated effort and the mastery of talents and abilities specific to your goals. Motivation and discipline, over time, give you the capacity to convert *possibility* into *probability.*

You'll remember that power is manifest by the 3 components of the *Power Triangle. Power* is the quantity of work in a specific time. *Power* is the result of your balanced, focused, and timely action. *Power,* expressed with controlled balance, focus and timing, converts *possibility* to *actuality.*

That's the whole philosophy of ***Dynamic Components of Personal Power****. That's it!*

So, what do you do first?

Earlier I referenced a tremendous lecture by Grandmaster Jhoon Rhee. Master Rhee came to America after living his younger years in war time Korea. He's now a philanthropist and an advocate for effective education in America based on the values and principles taught in martial arts. His "Joy of Discipline" program is now a landmark program for public schools in the Washington, D.C. area.

Master Rhee led us through a discussion of the age-old philosophical riddle "what came first, the chicken or the egg?" Imagine a room full of martial artists and business people arguing about whether the chicken or the egg was the source of poultry life as we know it! To be honest, it was a lot of fun.

The conclusion was simple: What difference does it make? Depending on how you look at it, the chicken might be the beginning of the egg; from that perspective, producing the egg may be the ultimate success in the life of the chicken.

If you look at things from the other end, the egg can be considered the beginning of the chicken. Once the chicken is hatched, the egg is successful in its end and the chicken begins its life, full of the promise of creating more eggs.

Ultimately, I seem to remember coming to a consensus that no matter where you decide to start the cycle, the chicken does represent a more *evolved* version of this life form. In that sense, you might say that the chicken has the grander capacity to experience life than the egg; relative to the talents and abilities of the chicken!

It might be worth asking yourself whether, at this point in your life, you consider yourself a chicken or an egg. At different points in life the answer may vary. Your answer may also be relative to a particular project or phase of life.

Wherever you're starting from, you can apply the Dynamic Components. I do, however, have a recommended order of application.

Whenever possible, start at the end and at the beginning at the same time. Be the chicken and the egg!

What the hell does that mean? It's much simpler than it sounds. Remember, you're the only person truly responsible for your success. You are in fact the beginning and the end of every endeavor you choose.

How to start at the end…

To really have control of your own destiny, it's essential that you develop a clear personal vision of success. You must make this vision completely real in your own mind.

There is an extremely powerful tool which can help you establish this vision it in your mind. This tool is *visualization.* The clearer you *visualize,* the more you can *realize.* Make your visualization as real as possible in your mind and you create a more tangible sense of your personal vision of success, providing a stronger level of motivation.

Some people find it very easy to visualize. You can simply sit and form a mental picture of what you'd like to accomplish. You can imagine yourself enjoying the fruits of your success by imagining yourself in your dream house or enjoying your vision of the perfect retirement.

Others might find it more difficult to produce actual mental imagery. I tend to be a more auditory person, so to stimulate the visualization process, I use actual pictures.

One of my ambitions is to tour the country presenting ***Dynamic Components*** seminars. I'm the consummate tourist, so I want to combine my work with plenty of time for sightseeing. To me, the best way to see America is on the road.

I've posted a picture of my dream motor home above my desk. Whenever I look at this picture, I find the motivation to plow through mundane tasks and do the work necessary to buy my motor home and get out on the road.

Of course, sitting and looking at the picture of my future tour bus isn't going to cause it to pull up to the curb in front of my house. In no way do I believe that belief and visualization alone will produce anything material or substantive, but without belief there is no possibility.

To increase the probability of success, you've got to convert the energy of thoughts and visualizations into action.

Visualization produces motivation and helps you see the reality of your goals. Many studies have shown that the more specific you can direct your thoughts; the more likely you are to produce tangible results. The more attention you pay to making your goals real in your mind, the more likely you are to manifest your success materially and physically.

So, create a goal and practice making your goal real first in your mind: start at the end.

Now let's go back to the beginning…

Action *requires* belief. No action will generate effective power without sufficient input energy. When we're talking about human life, this input energy is belief. You've got to know you can do it, or at least believe in your *ability* to do it, before you can do it! If you want to be a successful chicken, belief is your egg!

We all have the energy we need to achieve great success in life; we were born with it. Nature provides each of us with enough energy to change the world. To succeed we need to access this energy through the process of self-perfection. Self-perfection is the process of developing and applying personal power; personal faith and self-belief are the keys that open the door to this process.

We all want to be *successful*. However, each of us has a unique and personal definition of success. Your vision of success is completely up to you. Living is an art and the picture you paint is your life.

I don't consider the ***Dynamic Components*** to be a specific blueprint for success. I am not trying to specify your vision of success. You're the only person *responsible* for your success. You're the only person who can *define* your success. If you're interested in financial success, there are literally hundreds of systems available in that area. You have access to nearly limitless resources to help you become more successful in your spiritual or emotional life as well.

The ***Dynamic Components*** is a system for developing the resources you need to *power* your success. In order to make *any* system work, you've got to have sufficient power to get started, and to sustain your efforts…

Start by developing your personal power.

Experience has taught me that even as I *develop* personal power I become more successful. As I develop personal power I access the energy I need to power the systems available to me; and I use a lot of them!

Embarking on a goal or objective without personal power is like sailing with no wind. You're going to drift somewhere, but you have little or any control over where. You're likely to end up on the rocks, or adrift in an ocean of indecision, confusion and disappointment.

A self-improvement book like this one is only a tool. You've got to swing the hammer. Life is a *Do-It-Yourself* project!

I love to hear motivational speakers. I'm always amazed when some people leave an event saying, "That all sounds great, but I can't see myself doing these stupid exercises." OK, you made your choice! I've got a healthy skeptical streak in my personality; I pick and choose what works for me and those that suit my values, tastes and personality. However, I also know that when a successful person is sharing techniques with me that those techniques probably worked for at least one person: the person sharing the ideas. As long as I'm satisfied that a particular presenter is honest, I'm willing to keep my mind and heart open to the possibility that those techniques might work for me as well.

I also realize that *I'm* responsible for making any technique, system or idea work in my own life. I'm the one who has to supply the desire, the motivation, the discipline and the time.

Some people hope or think that if they simply sit, and well, think, that magically their thoughts will become material realities. I've already clearly stated my opinion in this regard; that expectation is, to use a kind expression, naïve.

It *is* powerful to learn to *go with the flow,* but if you think going with the flow is just like being a cork on the current you'll soon be in trouble. Every river runs to the sea, and the ocean is an awfully big place when you're just a cork.

Going with the flow means swimming *with* the current, rather than against it, whenever possible. Navigate the course toward your personal success with knowledge of the currents. Sorry to mix metaphors, but "don't spit into the wind."

Once you decide who you are and where you want to go, stop paddling upstream. Learn how to best apply your unique talents and opportunities to achieve your personal vision of success; *then do it!*

I recommend that you develop an over-arching personal definition of success; a *Master Plan.* Review the previous chapters as you start on this exercise. Post the *Power, Kung Fu* and *Energy Triangles* where you can see them. Keep an updated list of your current resources in the 3 major areas of life: material, emotional and spiritual. The *Triangles* are simply a map to show you the terrain. You're free to plot your own course.

There are some useful techniques to help you visualize success and stay focused on your master plan. *Let's look at few...*

One classic technique is to write your own eulogy. Each of us impacts the lives of many other people. What do you want people to say about you at your funeral? Imagine all your friends and the people you admire extolling your virtues and memorializing your achievements.

If that exercise is a little creepy for your tastes, assemble a collage of pictures representing your personal vision of success. Your collage might include a picture of your dream home, a place you'd like to retire, pictures of your children or loved ones, awards or testimonials. It's your life, you're the artist, create your own picture! You don't need to restrict yourself to places you've been, post up pictures of where you want to go. Post a photo of your *next* car, make up an award you'd *like* to have and put that on your wall. *Write your own testimonial.*

What's most important is to create and internalize a clear picture of what your success is going to look like.

Jack Canfield, author of the *Chicken Soup* books, teaches a fantastic technique in his book ***The Success Principles.*** As a personal motivation tool, Mr. Canfield took a marker and converted a dollar bill into a $100,000 note. He's not a forger; he used his imagination and a magic marker to create a $100,000 motivational tool. He pasted this modified note above his bed to remind him of his goal.

I loved this idea so I wrote myself a check for $501,000. My wife, Alex, put this check in a frame with a picture from one of our nicest vacations. I look at this check every day. Your purchase of my book is part of making this vision a reality. You have my sincere gratitude!

You've got to make sure any technique is comfortable for you. At first, I wrote my vision check for the round amount of $500,000. Something kept nagging at me until I remembered that I have a life insurance policy in the amount of $500,000. I was stuck on the idea that I could produce $500,000 in one day, at least for my wife, just by dying!

For now, I'd rather stick around and enjoy the hard earned fruits of my labor. I changed the amount and printed a new check. I learned that it's very important to make your vision absolutely positive!

Once again I'm going to warn against taking these exercises too literally. The point is to constantly keep your mind focused in a positive direction. Printing a bogus check for $501,000 has not, by itself, made me any richer. Looking at that check every day helps keeps me focused on my goals. That stupid check has helped me get up and out the door on many mornings when it would have been far easier to crawl back into bed and pull the covers over my head.

The picture of that check creates a reality in my mind that motivates me to keep working when I'm tired, to try again when I fail, and to keep my faith when I'm discouraged. At worst it sometimes just makes me smile; and some days a smile is worth a lot more than $501,000.

Martial artists use this process of visualization daily. To the initiated it probably looks as if we're crazy people jumping around in our pajamas. In our minds we're fighting real opponents; some of us think we can actually see them. Visualizing our movements with a "sense of enemy" brings intensity and clarity to our practice.

Dr. Dennis Waitley and others have tested the effects of visualization exercises on the performance of elite athletes. In these experiments, athletes are told to perform their specific sport only in their minds. Using extremely sophisticated monitoring techniques, they've found that even when completely still, the athlete's mind fires impulses to every muscle in the body needed to perform the sport. Athletes that practice visualization significantly increase actual physical performance.

This method works for every goal and objective we may have in the game of real life. We must start with an idea. The stronger our mental image is the stronger we will believe in the reality of that vision. The stronger we believe the more directed our action and the greater our probability of success.

My role as a kicker on my football team gave me a tremendous opportunity to experiment with these ideas. For those few of you who, as much as I find this hard to believe, may not be football fans, kickers are the funny little guys who run out to kick a field goal after the tough guys have sacrificed life and limb to get us in range!

Kicking a field goal is an intense mental exercise. There are a hundred things that can wrong, bad snap, bad hold, slippery turf, wind...Across the line of scrimmage and on the enemy sidelines your opponent will do his best to destroy your confidence. At the snap of the ball, some 3,000 pounds plus of angry humanity charges forth intent on your destruction.

When you're kicking to take the lead, especially when the game is on the line, the success and failure of every man on the team rides on your ability to focus and deliver a successful field goal.

In the middle of all this, *you gotta believe!* You've got to believe with your entire mind that your attempt will be successful.

There is no *close enough* in place kicking. The ball goes through the uprights, or it does not. This provides a very interesting laboratory where success and failure is clearly defined and easily measured.

I've made a careful study of my successful field goals and my misses. A successful kick is the direct result of absolute focus and the elimination of any negative thoughts. When I line up to kick, I've taught myself to ***expect success.*** I'm no longer *surprised* by a good kick; I'm surprised when I make a bad kick. *(I have been surprised when a bad kick went through!)*

Belief in the probability of success comes from practice.

Constant repetition and improvement are the keys to developing confidence. Confidence breeds success. Confidence comes from knowing that you've done everything you can do to produce your desired results, and this knowing is in direct proportion to your dedication to practice.

Most successful athletes use some technique to visualize performance and rehearse it in the mind before physically taking the field. Nobody talks to the place kicker before a field goal attempt! I have to remove myself from everything that's going on around me and simply establish the idea of the successful kick clearly in my mind. I've learned to apply this technique in business and personal life as well.

Establish a goal or objective. Take some time and just sit and think about how this goal will manifest itself in your life. Visualize it as if it's already done. Build a mental model of your success, just as an architect builds a mock-up of a skyscraper. Everything you do starts with an idea. Make your success real first in your mind and your actions will move more naturally in that direction.

There are hundreds of ways to practice this technique. Remember that your life is whole, not a pasted together assembly of separate parts. Success you manifest in one area of life benefits all the other areas of your life.

Practice success at play! Everyone spends some time at leisure activity. What you do with your leisure time can directly affect how successful you'll be. Choose activities that challenge the mind, body and spirit. Do things for fun that make you a better person. Spend time with other people who are focused on self-improvement and success.

For me, martial arts and football provide great opportunities to challenge myself and develop the habit of success. Every moment of every day is an opportunity to practice success. Of course, in real life, measuring success is not always as clearly defined as hitting or missing a field goal.

The ***Black Belt*** has become a universal symbol for success and excellence. This symbol is understood nearly everywhere inside and outside the martial arts world. This symbol, and others like it, serves the purpose of giving us a tangible object for positive thought and action. Any beginning martial artist can *visualize* standing in front of a mirror wearing a black belt. The black belt then becomes a powerful motivation for positive thought and action.

I do an exercise with my martial arts students below the rank of black belt. I have them close their eyes and visualize themselves as if looking in a mirror. I then tell them to transform their belts into black belts, *in their minds*. Next, I ask them to visualize performing their technique as if they are already *Black Belts*. I allow some time for the students to go through the entire routine mentally; then I tell them to open their eyes and do the technique as *Black Belts* would.

Every time we do this exercise there is a noticeable and distinct improvement in form and execution. That's the power of visualization. That's the power of a symbol.

Perfection is not a destination but rather a never ending process. Likewise, each success is not an end; it's a new beginning in a never ending adventure.

Your vision of success may change. You may achieve success in one area which leads you success in another. Some people achieve great material success, and then manage their material resources so they can benefit others. On the other hand, some people cultivate spiritual wealth that gives them a foundation for material success.

What is important is that we never stop the process. The priority of a particular need or desire may change. The most important thing to keep in mind is that each of us is a powerful and creative entity. It's our destiny to create, to achieve and to accomplish; then to share our success with others.

In most martial arts systems, once you achieve a certain level of skill and knowledge, it's your duty to share this skill and knowledge with others. Martial artists in the Japanese styles often use the word *Sensei* to honor teachers. *Sensei* literally means: *one who went before.* It's my responsibility as I become successful in martial skill to share this success with others. For some of us, teaching becomes our vocation.

The process is cyclical. One of the greatest challenges for any artist or craftsman is to transfer that skill to others. Sincere teachers and coaches usually find their greatest personal rewards in sharing their knowledge and skill with their students, sometimes far exceeding the rewards found in their own practice of their vocation.

Each of us can acquire only so much knowledge and skill in one lifetime. Sharing your knowledge and skill with others can influence lives long after you're gone. The knowledge and skill of one caring teacher can impact generations.

No matter how you define success, yours is always amplified by sharing that success with others. If you're a successful student, then teach. When you develop a particular skill, help others master that that skill. When you enjoy material success, put it to work to improve your community. In this way success is always multiplied and is always returned to you many times.

I have found one universal quality in sincerely successful people. Whenever I've met someone who is truly successful, this person is also truly *happy.* Happiness may be the best measurement and the best definition of success.

There are some other qualities I've found in happy and successful people. One of the most interesting is this…

Most happy and successful people I've met are extremely busy people.

Many people think that being busy causes stress; I disagree. It's not how much work you do, but rather *what* work you do that causes stress. Stress is caused by imbalance.

There's little stress when your work is in line with your personal vision of success. Find work that feels like play and you've got it made. I'm not saying that you'll never experience stress, but when you love your work, stress is the exception rather than the rule.

You'll certainly feel stressed if your work isn't balanced with the rest of your life. You'll be stressed out when your work doesn't reflect the true expression of your spirit. You'll be stressed when your work doesn't allow you to express your true talents and abilities, or when you see little chance of realizing your potential.

When your work supports your personal definition of success and genuinely makes you happy you'll be more relaxed, satisfied and healthy. This is the true meaning of the expression *going with the flow.*

Be careful, some people can be stressed out at play as much as they are at work! Doesn't gambling or substance abuse cause emotional, spiritual and physical stress? People who lead a runaway sex life or involve themselves in illicit affairs usually experience a high degree of stress. Others tax themselves materially by living beyond their means or by trying to maintain a lifestyle well over their heads.

Work that suits your emotional and spiritual personality opens up nearly inexhaustible supplies of energy. Leisure activities that nourish your mind, body and spirit energize your personal, professional and business life.

Action in and of itself doesn't cause stress. Life is action!

There's a powerful correlation between the life expectancy of a person who retires and what he does with retirement time. Those who volunteer, mentor and coach live much longer and happier lives than those removed from active lives. Senior housing and retirement communities now emphasize healthful and active lifestyles. Sedentary retirees have a greatly reduced life expectancy compared to those who maintain a vigorous physical, emotional and spiritual lifestyle.

Lack of productivity causes more stress than too much activity. Is it more stressful to be very busy doing a job you love or to be unemployed, broke and worried about the future?

Successful people *practice.* To a martial artist, everything is practice. It's what we do. There's no end to practice- only greater refinement and enjoyment. Practice is the incubator for competence, confidence, success and happiness. Practice is what you do, and continue to do, over time. Practice takes time; another reason to choose what you want to practice mindfully both at work and at play.

There's a dangerous expectation in today's culture: It's the expectation that everything must happen *NOW!* We want *everything now,* maybe even yesterday.

Have you heard the ads for pizza delivery in 30 minutes or less? We want our pizza so fast that we're willing to risk undercooked pizza and traffic accidents to satisfy our appetites. After a few accidents caused by high-speed pizza deliveries, some enlightened folks realized that it wasn't worth the risk.

Practice is the bridge between knowledge and skill. Remember that knowledge is not, in itself, power. You must direct knowledge through action to generate power. Over time, as you practice constant learning and focused action, you develop skill.

Practice takes time; this is the essence of the *Kung Fu Triangle.* We develop or embrace motivation in our minds, we set our bodies to action and maintain positive action through discipline and we continue this process over time.

Let me tell you how *I* would run a fast food restaurant. I'll call my restaurant *Sensei Jim's Kung Fu Burgers.* In a typical burger joint you pull up to the drive-through window and place your order. I imagine you're going to expect your burger to be ready when you pull around to the pick-up window, approximately a minute or two later, right?

At *Sensei Jim's Kung Fu Burgers* I'll greet you at the pick-up window with a big smile and say, "Drive around another 10,000 times; then you'll get your burger!"

That's the way *Kung Fu* works. Just imagine how good that burger is going to taste by the time you get it! Time is an important factor in true success. That may be part of the reason that lottery winners so often end up broke. True satisfaction comes from success earned through hard work, over time. *Only success earned is fully appreciated.*

Instant success is usually an illusion. Take the popular example of the singer who becomes an "overnight success." A singer may practice, work and perform for several years before suddenly being discovered by the public. The fact is that most apparent instant successes are built on years of dedicated practice that go unnoticed, and unappreciated, by the general public.

Watch the NFL draft and you'll see young men become instant millionaires...*instant?* How many years, how many hours, how much blood, sweat, tears, pain, doubt, fear, glory, defeat and victory lead up to this moment? No, there are no "instant" millionaires in professional sports. Being drafted by an NFL team is the culmination of a life-time of dedication to the practice of becoming a professional athlete.

And it's just the beginning! All great achievements take time, yet the only thing that lasts forever is the present moment. Once you can appreciate that success takes time, but the time is always now, you're on the road to mastery.

Again I'll emphasize the importance of *Beginner's Mind.* Start each day with a sense of wonder and exuberant curiosity. What opportunities do I have today? What can I learn today? Who will I meet, what will I see and where will I go today?

You *can* start each day slapping yourself on the back and congratulating yourself on your past accomplishments; or you can focus on the present and the potential available in this moment, in this day. The choice is yours. Everyone can be great in his or her own mind. There's nothing particularly harmful about thinking you're great from time to time, just don't let your greatness put an end to your process of self-perfection! If you aspire to greatness, you certainly have to start in the mind, but you also need to translate your thoughts into action to produce results.

I've met many *great* beginners in martial arts; these students are too willing to tell me how great they are.

When a student comes to me from another system, I'll usually ask if he's had some previous experience. I remember one such student who told me that after only 3 months of study in another style, his *Sensei* proclaimed him "the greatest natural fighter" he'd ever seen. I was honored to meet this man; given my own limited skills. I had no idea how I'd be able to help this guy, but I thought it would interesting to see what it was that made him so great. Maybe I could learn something!

After watching this guy perform for a few minutes I'd have to say, *not so much.*

I have not met all that many *great* black belts in my career. The best black belts don't worry about how great they are; they're more concerned with what they can do to become better. They'd rather hear about the other guy's accomplishments than talk about their own. They're curious about what the other guy can teach them. They want to know how to learn more and how to become better martial artists. Truly great black belts are first and foremost great students.

Successful people start each day looking for new ideas, new opportunities and new experiences. The past is a treasure, but it's done, ready to be put on the shelf and admired. The future is where the real reward lies and the future is being created ***now.***

When you meet someone who has been a black belt for a long time he'll often be wearing a frayed and tattered belt. It's may be the first black belt he ever received.

When I earned my first black belt rank, my Master gave me a special belt: very heavy, dark black. He told me that if I continued my study and practice that over the years, I'd be tying and untying that belt thousands of times. He told me never to wash my belt; that the belt should keep all the blood, sweat and tears I would shed over years of practice. He said if I treated my belt this way it would become worn, and the cover would fray.

My belt is now fashionably distressed. The original rich, dark black has faded to gray. The black exterior layer is worn and torn and exposes an inner core; this core is white. As many of you may know, the white belt is the belt worn by beginners.

Each time I tie on my belt, the fading black tells me where I am now, the white core reminds me of where I started and where I can still go, provided I always keep the mind and spirit of the beginner.

The longer I continue my life as a martial artist the more I become aware of the power of the sense of wonder, curiosity and enthusiasm we all have as beginners. Tying my belt is a powerful ritual that helps me keep *Beginner's Mind.*

I remember the belt worn by Professor Nick Cerio. Professor Cerio is renowned in *Kenpo* circles. I had the opportunity to work with him on perhaps two or three occasions, for just a few hours each time. In this short time he had a profound effect on my practice and later on my teaching.

His tattered and torn black belt seemed to hang on by just a few threads. I remember one of his assistants joking with him, "Professor, when are you going to get a new belt?" His response seemed to be part of a well rehearsed routine and he responded, best as I can remember, by saying that when he died, they better put him in the box with this same belt!

As far as I know they did!

The best teachers in my life personify the wonder of *Beginner's Mind.*

Successful people don't confuse success with satisfaction.

I have had very satisfying moments during times when I would not say I was particularly successful. I've also had some wonderful successes that seemed to lack any tremendous feeling of satisfaction, at the time. This problem used to be very confusing to me. Shouldn't I be satisfied after a particular success? From my own experience I'd have to say, *not necessarily.*

I'm a very busy person, and I enjoy what I do. I consider myself very fortunate. Even in moments of poverty or loneliness I'd have to say that I've usually had much to be thankful for. I am generally a very happy person. *I'm not usually satisfied!*

I consider my lack of satisfaction a blessing; my lack of satisfaction provides motivation to continually seek greater challenges. When there is a void, there is potential.

One of my life goals is to finish my life unfinished! Like one of my greatest heroes, Benjamin Franklin, I want to continue to learn and grow and develop myself until they put me in the ground. I can't imagine ever being fully satisfied; however, in any moment I can *choose* to be happy.

Start by clearly defining your personal vision of success. Be open to change. Develop a positive attitude and keep your vision in the face of challenges and failures. Learn from your failures and make them part of your success.

Cultivate your resources in *body, mind* and *spirit.* Access these resources to develop power through *motivation* and *discipline* over *time.* Apply this power with proper *balance, focus* and *timing.*

As you enjoy success keep ***Beginner's Mind*** and ask yourself what's next. In this way each small success will build toward ultimate success: a happy and productive life full of power and energy you will share with others. As you share with others, you are recycling the energy you constantly access to create your own personal power and success.

This cycle is abundant, everlasting and is accessible in every present moment. This is the great cycle of life, and life is now.

The Spirit of Power

Student: *Why, when we're born, is our first sound one of sadness?*

Master: *Is it?*

Student: *When we're first born we cry!*

Master: *Of course! Until birth you're part of your mother. You live within your mother, connected in every way and fully dependent. When you're born, you're separated from your mother and start your independent life, alone for the first time, without sight and without understanding. Of course you'll cry!*

Student: *Then we're destined for sadness?*

Master: *Are we? What happens once the baby is placed in the arms of the mother? The baby quiets, the mother and everyone attending the birth smiles. The baby soon learns to smile. The baby's smile brings happiness to everyone around him. This happiness reconnects the baby with the mother and begins to connect the baby with other people.*

Student: *So the purpose of happiness is connection.*

Master: *The purpose of life is happiness. Our spirit connects us with one another and with our purpose. Our purpose is happiness, and happiness is the true expression of our nature and spirit.*

I hope I've earned some of your trust, because in this chapter it's time to talk about two of the most contentious subjects known to humanity: *money and God.*

I don't have the right to define your personal success. I don't know how much money or what possessions define your idea of success; that's your business. In the area of spirituality I feel even less capable of defining your personal vision of success. I do know that to be truly successful and happy we all need to develop our spiritual resources.

For many of you I'm sure your religious practice is central to your spiritual development and fulfillment. Others may be struggling to find some sense of spiritual identity. Some may be searching for a spiritual practice, or a community which fulfills needs the need for spiritual connection and development.

I've also met several self-professed atheists who claim no spiritual affiliation whatsoever; some of them are extremely successful, happy, and fulfilled. Each time I've met a truly happy and successful atheist I've found this person to be truly powerful and balanced *spiritually.* Each of these people had some self-styled philosophy or personal belief structure that fulfilled the fundamental human need for spirituality.

It's not my place to judge anyone's personal philosophy or particular spiritual viewpoint; I'll only state that every truly successful and happy person I meet practices some system of what I would call spiritual development. Once the semantic arguments are sorted out, the devout person and the atheist both employ the same ***Dynamic Components*** to achieve success and happiness.

Your personal spiritual perspective defines the character of your spiritual identity. Your expression of personal power is directed by this spiritual self-image. See yourself with a caring and generous spiritual nature, and you're more likely to apply power to create positive results in your life, and the lives of others.

The application of power, above almost any other form of human expression, defines a person's character and reveals a person's true spirit. It's easy to see why so many people believe the cliché, "Power corrupts, and absolute power corrupts absolutely"...*It can!* However, *you* have the power to decide whether power will corrupt your life, or whether you'll use power to improve your life and the world around you. You control your spiritual development and you control the spirit of your personal power.

A person who expresses personal power positively is characterized by a positive spirit and energy. One of the most powerful expressions of a positive spirit is generosity. If you want to achieve true success, if you want to get, you have to give. You've got to give in all three areas of life: *material, emotional* and *spiritual.*

The logical argument would be that many selfish people become successful. No, they don't, not as we've been defining genuine success. I have met selfish people who have a lot of money; I don't remember meeting any selfish people who are truly happy. Money alone cannot buy happiness; that's one cliché that is absolutely true!

Another danger is that one can be *materialistic* emotionally, and spiritually. Spiritual and emotional materialism is when *possession,* even possession of the intangible, becomes more important than the *process* of self-perfection.

Many years ago Lao Tzu taught…

"Produce but do not possess.
Act without expectation.
Advance without dominating.
These are called the Subtle Powers."

True success is not about possession. I've been clear in my belief that to be successful and happy we need to have enough. You define how much *enough* is *enough,* but you do need *enough* money, *enough* love, *enough* companionship, belief and faith. If you feel lacking in any of these areas it's nearly impossible to feel successful and happy.

To be happy and successful you've got to generate some wealth; you need to build your resources. These resources include money, knowledge, fame and goodwill.

Then you've got to learn how to put those resources to work through sharing and investing. By investing I don't mean just the Wall Street version, but rather to stake some of your resources on the talents and abilities of others. The greatest investment you can make in another person is trust.

Hoarding treasure always diminishes its power.

Jesus told a story about three servants entrusted with the care of their master's gold. The first is given three bags, the second two and the third, one bag of gold.

While the master is away, the first two invest the gold. When the master returns, these guys are able to present their master with double the amount he left in their care. The third servant buried the gold to keep it safe. He opted for the lowest degree of risk, and of course, his return was proportional.

The first two servants understood the ***Dynamic Components*** and put them to work! They used their *knowledge resources* to invest the *material resource* of the master's gold. They acted *courageously* and *focused* on abundance. They were *motivated* to please their master. They were *disciplined;* they did not gamble the money, they invested it with skill.

Most of all, they understood that in order to achieve results, *they needed to take action.* Power is the measure of results and results are produced through action.

The third guy just wanted to play it safe! His actions were dictated by fear and poverty. He took what he thought to be the safest and easiest course, but this wasn't a course of action, it was a course of fear and complacency.

There's another, deeper message here: the master trusted his servants with his treasure. He had no guarantee that he'd return to find his treasure intact, much less increased. His servants might have taken advantage of the opportunity to squander all his money on the ancient versions of sex, drugs and *Rock & Roll.* The safer and easier option might have been to take his gold with him.

Instead he chose to *give.* He gave the servants his *trust.* He invested his trust in his servants. If you expect to gain anything you have to *give. You don't gain by just hanging on.*

Buddhists express this philosophy through the "Principle of Non-Attachment."

When we're obsessed with the possession itself, then we can't help but be disappointed, or even angry, if we lose it. When we covet, we create jealously. When we allow jealously and anger to dominate our thinking, we create aggression and even violence. We become takers rather than givers.

I'm not a hypocrite and I won't say that money doesn't buy happiness. Ultimately, it doesn't, but money and material wealth *can,* when used properly, eliminate a lot of problems that cause unhappiness.

More important than any material possession to me is the experience of the work I've done to earn that possession. A new car is only new for a short time; the skills and talents I developed to earn my new car can serve me for the rest of my life. I think about it this way:

I don't base my happiness on anything that can be taken away from me!

This is not an idea I'm asking you to believe just because I'm taking the time to include it in this book. It works for me, all I'm asking you to do is to think about this point of view and consider how this principle works in your life and in the world around you.

Have you *ever* enjoyed true happiness by taking? Have you ever *truly* gained happiness from someone else's suffering? You may experience *satisfaction* through aggression, anger, jealousy and violence; but never true happiness. *(Ironic stuff coming from someone who enjoys fighting and football, eh?)*

"Never mistake my kindness for weakness, or my silence for ignorance."

The fact is that true kindness and compassion are only expressed from a position of power. First of all, you can't share what you don't have. Second, most people who are corrupted by power are those who are actually the least powerful personally. People easily corrupted by power are those people who think that what they possess and who they control are the truest measures of their success.

Truly successful people understand that success comes from having control over one's own life and destiny. Success is expanded through generosity and sharing, not by attempting to control others. True success isn't the result of controlling other people and things; it's the result of practicing true self-control.

Possessions do not in themselves have any power; they are only symbols of what you've achieved. "You can't take it with you" is a very wise proverb. In the beginning, and in the end, not one of us really *owns* anything. We're really just temporary stewards of the material possessions we enjoy during our lifetimes.

Does this mean it's wrong to accumulate material riches? I don't think so! I've come to believe the complete opposite. I do want to accumulate material resources; I have material goals as part of my personal vision of success. However, I understand that these resources are merely *on loan* to me during my lifetime. I'm grateful for the resources I'm able to enjoy and feel a sense of obligation to pass these resources, intact and increased, to the next generation of people who can enjoy them in turn.

A misguided dedication to poverty as a method of spiritual salvation is as problematic as greed and selfishness. Your personal definition of success may be very modest in terms of material needs or desires. Still, unless you want to be dependent on others, you'd better include a plan to provide *enough* of whatever you feel you need throughout your life.

What happens when you don't have enough? At some point you'll have to turn to others to provide for you. In our culture many people feel *entitled* to some sort of help from others, at least at some point in life.

This entitlement mentality is bankrupting our society, both materially and spiritually. There's the obvious problem that the entitlement stream is so grossly inflated that local, state and federal treasuries are going bankrupt. The deeper problem is that entitlement, when abused, destroys self-reliance. Too many people are trapped in a desperate cycle of poverty encouraged by a new ideology of apathy and hopelessness.

There's nothing wrong with accepting charity when it's truly needed, but there is a vast difference between a hand-up and a hand-out. Charity benefits both the donor and the recipient when it's given with the spirit of selflessness and accepted with the spirit of gratitude.

If you really want to develop power in your life, use the resources available to you, *all of them.* Just be sure to use these resources to cultivate personal power. Take great care not to get trapped in an endless cycle of dependency materially, emotionally, or spiritually.

The sad truth is that when it comes to material resources, many of us have squandered at least part of our youth. When I was young I felt as if I had plenty of time to worry about money, later. My age of enlightenment dawned at around my fortieth year; I've got a lot of catching up to do.

I met a man at one of my seminars who was facing the loss of a job at age 60. He lived a tremendous life as a biologist. His adventures were worthy of consideration for a *National Geographic* special! As we talked about balance, he experienced a personal revelation: He realized that he was facing big trouble; he was extremely fearful of where his life was going because he did nothing in his youth to provide for his material resources for later in life. He didn't need a lot of money to be happy, but now he was facing the loss of his career with few prospects for future work and no material resources to support even a modest lifestyle in retirement. He did not provide for the future while he was young; and he suddenly realized his future is now.

There are people who live happy and successful lives with very little personal material wealth. Some of these people, however, create and control incredible material resources and direct these resources to benefit others. Mother Theresa did not have keep money for herself, but her work inspired the generosity of millions of people throughout her lifetime. Her actions raised millions, if not billions of dollars throughout her lifetime, which she and those working with her directed toward incredible works of charity. The Dalai Lama requires very little in the way of personal possessions, yet his thoughts and actions drive a media empire that provides for the material needs of a complete culture of people living in exile.

Bill Gates, Oprah Winfrey and Ted Turner more closely fit the mold of the classic American millionaire. They each enjoy what most of us would consider extremely privileged lives, yet each of them shares incredible material, intellectual and spiritual resources on a scale most of us can only imagine.

Is there anything wrong with Oprah enjoying some of the billions of dollars her actions have attracted to her life? She created her material and spiritual wealth from a background of poverty and abuse, and she obviously recognizes the power of sharing that wealth with others.

Conversely, is self-imposed poverty necessarily the key to spiritual fulfillment? Would Oprah be such a powerful force in the lives of so many people had she accepted poverty or weakness?

Let's leave money behind for a while and talk about emotional and spiritual wealth. Just as we need enough material resources to support our definition of success, we also need to develop resources in our emotional and spiritual lives in order to enjoy true happiness.

Happiness is the result of abundance. Depression is the condition of poverty.

Just as in material life, there are those who are very wealthy in emotional and spiritual resources. There are also those who are possessive, greedy and selfish.

In emotional life it's fairly easy to understand greed and selfishness. Everyone knows at least one "emotional vampire." The *emotional vampire* steals energy and power just like the vampire in a horror movie sucks blood from a victim's neck.

The vampire is the mythological icon for greed and selfishness. He kills for his own sustenance, yet can never be satisfied. His reward is immortality, yet he's a prisoner of darkness and can never fully experience life. He's a symbol of hedonism yet he's completely dependent on the suffering of others to sustain his own life.

Emotional vampires work the same way. Modern science calls this condition "co-dependency." This is not the healthful "inter-dependence" that Stephen Covey talks about, but rather a complete state of reliance on others, taking, never really giving.

What kind of life is this? Have you ever been an emotional vampire? In my experience most of us have been, or at some time in life will, be an emotional vampire. Hopefully as an emotionally powerful person you'll learn to recognize this condition when it happens and correct your actions before you become a pain in the neck.

The problem with emotional vampirism is that you continually drain those around you. An emotional vampire has to keep moving from victim to victim, and never finds true success in any friendship or relationship. This person always finds fault in others and never accepts responsibility for his own condition and circumstances.

Develop independence through personal power, and by sharing power with others. Associate with people who understand the importance of individual power and respect interdependency. Rather than *taking* from one another, a group of interdependent people *accept* the gifts offered by others. Accepting in contrast to taking produces feelings of gratitude and appreciation rather than feelings of obligation or debt.

The most profound expressions of the power of giving are those of love and respect. Love and respect are the two most important points of human emotional contact and serve as the bridges for emotional and spiritual connection between people.

I'm not talking here about romantic love associated with sexual attraction. You could reduce romantic love to a biochemical process of our instinctive drive to reproduce; the spiritual expression of love is about *compassion.* It's about acknowledging the value of another human being and appreciating common humanity. Love is the recognition of my *self* in others. Love is extending my *self* to others because it is the right and natural way for human beings to treat one another.

Respect is taking care of this relationship and connection we have with others.

"Respect is love in plain clothing."

It's natural to feel love for other human beings. It is appropriate to express respect at any time. The source of all love and respect resides with the spirit.

I told you at the beginning of this chapter that we were going to talk about two volatile subjects: money and God. First we talked about one; here's the other!

At the risk of becoming really repetitive, it's not up to me to define your personal success in any area, least of all in the area of spirituality. What I'm trying to do is identify the basic components used by all successful and happy people, and hopefully present them in a way you can apply readily in your personal and professional life.

I sincerely hope that my ideas are not offensive to anyone's particular religious or spiritual beliefs. I am satisfied in my mind and heart that they shouldn't be. Still, whenever we discuss religion there is the potential for disagreement, offense and conflict.

Your personal religious beliefs are your own business. In my life I've met with and talked with people from dozens of various religious affiliations. It's kind of cliché to say "I have a friend who's a (fill in the blank)," but it's true. I have friends that are Christian, Jewish and Muslim; Buddhist, Hindu and atheist. I've met Satanists, Wiccans, Druids and Pagans. I have friends in nearly every major Christian sect and some who practice Native American and tribal religions.

You might say I'm a bit of a religion and philosophy junky. I've read about and studied something about every religion and philosophy I've ever heard about. I'm looking forward to learning about many more.

I've even developed a fascination with why people are attracted to *cults*. Why are people attracted to philosophical or religious practices that direct them toward isolation and negativity, even sometimes violence and self-destruction?

We all have a need to be connected to other human beings. We also feel some need to understand our place in the universe. The problem is that the universe is too big for us to fully comprehend, and a human lifespan provides far too little time for a comprehensive study! That's why we all have an instinctive need for some spiritual connection. Psychologists now believe that this desire for spiritual connection is hard-wired in the deepest chambers of the human psyche.

All I'm saying is that there is much about life, nature, and if you wish, God, that we don't understand. We don't know why the good sometimes die young and evil people sometimes seem to go on forever. We don't understand why we feel cursed when a tornado destroys our home and blessed when it misses us, even if it destroys the other guy's home.

I can only talk about *spirit* in the context of *feelings,* and feelings really can't be argued about intelligently. You have your feelings and I have mine. Yours may differ from mine. We can't weigh a feeling. We really can't measure a feeling outside the language of poetry or music.

We really don't even know when life starts, or the exact moment it ends. We talk of the mind, but nobody has ever taken a picture of one. We talk of the soul, but nobody really knows what it is. We talk about life after death but we don't know by personal experience whether or not *I* will be after I die and if so, what form or existence *I* will take.

We really don't even fully understand the distinction between *I* and *We,* so who am I to pretend to tell you about spiritual wealth? What, in turn, can you tell me?

What really matters is this: Somehow, most of the time, even the least faithful of all of us holds some hope for tomorrow. Tomorrow has no more material substance than the mind or the soul, but it provides our entire reason for continuing to be here today. As human beings, we can't imagine a fate much worse than the loss of some hope for tomorrow.

I don't know which way you'll choose to reconcile yourself with nature, the universe, or God, but I do know we all have the innate desire for this reconciliation. You are a part of something bigger than yourself; the problem is nobody knows exactly what you're a part of, however…

We know instinctively how to connect with that which is bigger than we are. This connection is made through *feeling.* *Spiritual practice* is how we this develop this connection. Spiritual practice helps make that which is bigger than our understanding more acceptable. Spirituality helps us find comfort in the idea that while human existence is temporary and maybe even insignificant in the big picture, some meaning in this existence is still valuable and important to each of us as tiny humans trying to deal with who we are here and now.

As vast as the universe is, as far as we know there is no other you. As much as we're all the same, we're all also a unique expression of life in this particular time and space.

Holy cow!

This is really important. At the very beginning of the book I asked you to accept the truth that your success starts with only you. You're the only person responsible for your success.

Many people want proof, or results, before they're willing to put in the work. The universe, well, just doesn't work that way. You have to put in the work to produce the results.

Why should you put in the work?

You gotta have faith!

When you start to accept the fact that as small as you are in the universe you are also very important, you can start to have faith in yourself. This faith is the cornerstone of success. Faith and personal belief is the fundamental source of human energy. Without faith there is no reason for action. You've got to believe that there is probably going to be a tomorrow, and that you'll have a meaningful role in it, in order to move yourself to action.

The way to cultivate faith and renew your energy is through spiritual practice, and there are plenty to choose from. Many of you will develop your own personal practice. I won't be the judge; I have enough work to do to judge my own actions.

I will risk imprinting my own personal belief on your definition of spiritual practice in one regard. Make your practice ***positive.*** Spirituality is the mechanism through which we develop our sense of good and evil and how we express good and evil in the world around us. Your spiritual practice is your system for living a good, productive and happy life.

I don't think it's difficult to tell the difference between good and evil. You shouldn't always go by *if it feels good, do it,* but you can make the assumption that if it feels good now, and is likely to continue to feel good for a long time, it's probably OK. If your thoughts and actions promote your own development, contribute to human progress in general, and cause no intentional or knowing harm to others, you're probably on the right track.

If your thoughts and actions don't feel right, if you feel guilt, negativity, depression and isolation, you better pay attention. If what you're doing now feels great, but you know you're going to pay for it tomorrow or in the future, you better pay attention. If you don't know *how* you're going to pay for it, you better pay attention! If what you're doing is obviously harmful to yourself or others, or if you even think it might be, you're probably going down the wrong path.

Sometimes the issue of good and evil can be complex, but that's usually on a grander scale. The people who discovered fossil fuels didn't intend to ruin the environment. Historically, changing from coal to oil cleaned up most of the major industrial cities of the 18th Century. Gas and oil changed human life forever, and most of the trade and interaction we have with people of different cultures today would not be possible without this technology.

Today we understand that our use of fossil fuels can be harmful. Now it's time to invent a better and cleaner way to get around and heat and light our world. So, are oil companies good or evil? When you drive to the store or heat your home with oil, are you good, or evil?

The answer lies in aligning ourselves with the greater good and focusing our efforts in that direction. That's the power of spirituality in a timely and practical example. We're more likely to tend toward goodness when we appreciate our connection to the universe and other beings.

It is our nature to act with goodness, that's why it usually feels right. Most of us get in trouble when we act against our nature.

When we have faith that our thoughts and actions are important to those around us and to the future we tend to act with more diligence. When we have faith we act in ways that will improve life, now and for the future.

The greatest source of human energy is one we can't weigh or measure with any scientific equipment. The greatest and most fundamental source of human energy is the human spirit.

We need to cultivate and develop our spirit in order to develop and maintain faith. We need faith to sustain our efforts toward success and happiness. The way to develop spirit is through spiritual practices and by nurturing our connection to nature and to one another. The way to sustain faith is through the application of spiritual practices in daily life.

Most of all, the development of the human spirit is dependent upon challenges. As we face and overcome challenges we condition ourselves for success, now and in the future. Dealing with adversity is weight lifting for the spirit.

On any given day, chances are that you will be here to face tomorrow. There will be some challenges tomorrow; there will also be opportunities.

Tack this to your bulletin board:

"I welcome the opportunity to test my skills against such a worthy opponent."

Adversity is a worthy opponent; welcome his challenge with courage and spirit and you've greatly increased your chances for success.

Once again: Simple...not easy!

Failure: Know Your Enemy!

Despite your best efforts and intentions, you will sometimes fail. In fact, your road to success might be paved with failure after repeated failure. I've used most of this book to paint an optimistic picture. *It's time for a reality check.*

The more I learn about success the more I run into one immutable fact:

"Successful people fail."

Let that little factoid sink in. *Successful people FAIL...much of the time!* Thomas Edison, one of the proverbial icons of modern success reported over 2,000 failed attempts to invent the electric light bulb.

Tom Brady was relegated to 2nd string position in both college and pros before his talents were recognized. A lot of people considered him a two time failure. He used every slight as motivation; he used his time to perfect his skills. He was ready when opportunity eventually came, and he led the New England Patriots to 3 Super Bowl titles *(and counting).*

Study great stories of success and you'll see for yourself that failure is an essential ingredient. Most of the people you think of as successful have experienced challenges, ordeals, personal suffering; sometimes poverty, and always some failure along the way.

There are some major differences between successful people and those who sink into failure quicksand:

Successful people always learn something from failures. To a successful person, failures are fertilizer for success.

Once a failure is recognized and the lesson learned, successful people let it go. They don't beat themselves with failure, they move on to the next opportunity.

Successful people apply the ***Dynamic Components of Personal Power.*** They build their power resources in *body, mind* and *spirit.* They cultivate power through *motivation* and *discipline* over *time.* They apply power with *balance, focus* and *timing.*

Successful people maintain a positive attitude, even in the face of adversity and hardship; even when everyone else is negative.

Successful people never quit.

The Apollo 13 astronauts faced nearly insurmountable odds when their spacecraft exploded. They were losing oxygen and electrical power. They had no heat, little light to work by, and had to fly most of the mission without a guidance computer.

As the situation reached the darkest hours, Flight Director Gene Krantz assembled his team and gave them this directive:

"Failure is not an option!"

That's ultimate Failure with the capitol "F."

During one of my frequent episodes of stupidity, I tried an abortive career as an amateur boxer. In the very short time I knew him my trainer, Dave Marquis, made quite an impact on my philosophy and my nose.

A fighter condenses all the trials of life into a very compact space and time. The visceral challenge of the ring breeds some insightful ringside philosophers, and Dave was one of the best. One night, after having my faced bashed into a bloody pulp, Dave said, "Don't worry, you always learn more when you lose!" Sage advice!

Then he added, "But some days you just don't feel like learning anything!" Too true! You'll have your days of triumph and you can, if you choose, relax a little on those days. On those other days, convert those losses into lessons which become part of future victories.

Successful people don't *accept Failure;* they just recognize failure as part of the game. Whether or not failure is absolute is usually a matter of choice. Of course, in life just as in boxing, failure can be painful.

Human beings are wired to avoid pain and seek pleasure. It does seem as if nature has a sense of humor. Real success always seems to be paid for with some misery. That opening to the old TV sports show *Wide World of Sports* probably should have been: "the thrill of victory and the agony of...*victory!"*

Enjoy the good feeling that comes with achievement. These brief moments of joy are usually hard to hold on to. I think that's why the ancient philosophers instruct us *not* to try to hold on to these moments. Simply enjoy the moment, let go, and move on to the next challenge.

Martial artists like to talk about becoming "one with the enemy." Knowing your enemy is one of most important keys to success. Who is the enemy standing in the way of your success?

Your worst enemy is usually the same person who brushes your teeth in the mirror every day. I'm sure you've heard the words "You are your own worst enemy."

Make "Failure is not an option" a personal motto. Make a conscious choice to rise above failure. Failure sometimes happens; success is what you do with it. Devote yourself to the cultivation of Personal Power and you constantly improve the probability of success.

Let's take another reality check:

There are sometimes events and conditions outside our control.

Of course, some people preach that by your thoughts, you attract *everything* that happens to you. You do attract *much* of what happens to you, maybe even *most* of what happens to you, but there are some things you can't do anything about.

You are not God. Do you control tornados, hurricanes, lightning storms or falling trees? You can be the victim of a crime, laid off from your job, or wake up in a country at war without having done anything to deserve that fate. There are hazards in the real world above and beyond your control and influence.

No matter how devastated, successful people prevail through these events and conditions. Successful people *"get themselves up, dust themselves off, and start all over again!"*

Soichiro Honda failed several times to win a contract to supply piston rings to the Japanese market before World War II. He eventually won his contract; before he could enjoy his success, his factory was bombed…twice.

After surviving the war, his rebuilt factory was again destroyed by an earthquake. Honda had no insurance, and Japan was suffering from a terrible shortage of nearly everything needed to build a manufacturing plant.

At the same time a terrible gasoline shortage made the bicycle Japan's primary mode of transportation. Honda chose to turn disaster into opportunity. He invented a small engine to power bicycles. He shook off the dust, convinced over 5,000 bicycle shop owners to make small investments, and became one of the world's most successful entrepreneurs.[26]

In a few more years, an American energy "crises" would provide Honda with the opportunity to conquer the Western automobile market. When most people saw only scarcity; Honda saw an opportunity to build a car that would go farther on less fuel. The rest, as they say, is history.

Most of my heroes are people who faced incredible challenges and became the shapers of our society. Most of the people who shaped our society faced incredible challenges.

When you face failure, give it a new name or let it go. The only thing you need to carry from a failure is a lesson. By the way, after getting the Apollo 13 astronauts back to earth safely, NASA classified that mission a "successful failure."

The secret is courage. Have the courage to welcome failure as a worthy adversary against whom you can test your skill. When others see failure as the end, see failure as the beginning. When others see disaster, look for opportunity.

When you're at the end of your rope, start climbing!

I do try not to repeat the same mistake too often. The only way to avoid repeating mistakes is to learn from them. Repeating the same mistakes again and again isn't perseverance, that's stupidity!

As long as you're learning, growing, and moving forward, your failures help build your capacity to succeed. Failure is part of your power generating process. Remember always that power isn't how hard you're working; it's the measure of the results you produce from your work.

Thomas Edison, after all those "failed" attempts to invent the light bulb said:

"Results! Why, man, I have gotten a lot of results. I know several thousand things that won't work."

That's powerful!

If successful people fail so much of the time, how many times do unsuccessful people fail? Now *that's* an interesting question, and I've given it a great deal of thought.

So, how many times* do *unsuccessful people fail?
Answer: Usually not more than once.

Think about it. Successful people see opportunity in every disaster; unsuccessful people see disaster in every opportunity!

The vocabulary of the unsuccessful person is:

- **I can't.**
- **I shouldn't.**
- **I couldn't.**
- **I wouldn't.**

Unsuccessful people seldom fail because they seldom take any chances. They take the safe road, even when that road is boring them to death. Success involves risk; the safe road is the road to mediocrity.

Your success is relative to your needs, your desires, your ambitions and your sense of achievement and abundance.

When you want more for of anything, you've got to put something on the line to get it. Too many people say they want more, but then do nothing to further their cause. Too many people say they're satisfied, but spend a lot of time bitching about life. To those people I say stop bitching and get living!

You need to distance yourself from negative people! That may sound cold, but these are the people who will tell you that you can't and you shouldn't. Negativity is contagious; *get away from them!*

Back to Thomas Edison; he decided to invent a talking machine to record and play back the human voice. Friends and experts told him it would be impossible. Their reasoning: it had never been done before!

If he had listened to the doubters, we might still be shouting through cardboard megaphones and taking shorthand.

Every great thing that anyone has ever accomplished had, at one time, never been done before.

Negative people are personal power vampires. Given the opportunity they'll suck ambition right out of your veins.

I'm not saying you should surround yourself with people who only agree with you. Intelligent, sincere and rational advice can prevent disaster. You *should* seek advice and counsel when you're making major decisions. A *master mind group* can be very helpful in planning your success strategy.

It's also important not to confuse a difference of opinion with negativity. You shouldn't dismiss advice as negative just because it's different than what you had in mind. Sometimes people who have already walked the walk can smooth the path and prevent you from making the same mistakes they did. You should be open to change and ready to incorporate sound advice.

Just be certain to seek advice from people honest enough to disagree with you rationally when appropriate, and those who will support you once you've made your decision.

Before we descend into one of those *you can do anything you set your mind to* pep talks let me be very clear about my own personal philosophy of success.

The *Black Belt* is, to martial artists, an important symbol of personal excellence. For any student willing to do what it takes to become a *Black Belt,* I will make two promises, and only two: First, if you're willing to do what it takes to become a *Black Belt,* you will, within the scope of your talents and abilities, be able to do anything you want in your life. Second, you'll learn how to recognize and develop your own unique talents and abilities.

The practice of martial arts is extremely introspective. We constantly access our progress, seek the criticism of instructors, and embrace the never ending process of self-perfection. Lost in many contemporary martial arts practices is the idea that eventually the process will become more important than any particular goal. In other words, the process of self-perfection becomes more important the end result of perfecting anything.

Once you understand how to analyze your own strengths and weaknesses, you can develop and apply personal power to achieve any goal within the scope of your current strengths, and the limits of your current weaknesses. Develop personal power and you also develop the capability to work on improving weaknesses and fortifying strengths. Through this process you accomplish everything a human being can be expected to accomplish; constant self-improvement.

Could the process of constant self-perfection actually be the true meaning of life?

I've heard worse suggestions! People who dedicate their lives to constant self-perfection are also those who consider life *meaningful.* Improve yourself and your life is more likely recognized as meaningful to others.

The true enemies of success and self-perfection are the people, conditions, and circumstances that stand in the way of this process. Still, we can't control the thoughts and actions of others; we can only control our own thoughts and actions.

Once again, our most dangerous enemies are those that exist within our own hearts and minds.

Here are the big three. Let's call this ***The Destructive Triangle:***

- ✍ **Doubt**
- ✍ **Fear**
- ✍ **Complacency**

I fear complacency the most. Complacency is fertile ground for doubt and fear!

Doubt *is sometimes* the result of internalizing *genuine* failures. Self-doubt is sometimes pounded into us by people who influence our early development. Some people carry genuine doubt as a result of conditions beyond one's control such as natural disasters, disease, and physical or emotional trauma.

HOWEVER…For every disaster, wherever there's legitimate poverty and hardship, there are always great stories of triumph. We're always the most fascinated by stories about people who face the most incredible challenges and succeed against all odds. We have a name for these people: we call them ***Heroes.***

Success comes from how you choose to deal with the cards you've been dealt. You may not be able to control external conditions; you can *always* choose your response.

Your positive mental attitude is the best defense against the negativity of others. Positive mental attitude gives you the ability to act with courage in the face of life's greatest challenges, and to keep going when others would quit.

Be careful, however; sometimes complacency can disguise itself as positive emotional state. Don't mistake the true meaning contained in the world's great teachings, as many do, by assuming that a positive mental and spiritual state is the *only* requirement for success. Taken to an extreme, some people ignore medical attention for serious illnesses; some squander fortunes on cults and predatory gurus.

As you can probably tell, I'm a champion of personal responsibility. I believe that nature provides us with unlimited power and abundance. I also believe that it's my own responsibility to develop the intellectual, emotional and spiritual capacity to recognize and access this power and abundance.

Without personal responsibility, it's very difficult to recognize opportunity. Unless you're willing to extend your own hand and open your own heart, it's difficult to recognize and appreciate the gifts endowed by nature and offered by the generous people you encounter in life.

Dr. Yang, Jwing-Ming is well known in the martial arts world as a sincere and brilliant teacher. I'm extremely grateful for his profound influence on my life and work.

As a martial artist and a scientist Dr. Yang has done much to bridge the ancient and modern, the *physics* and the *metaphysics,* of many of these ancient practices. He is instrumental in bringing a new understanding of the practical applications of arts such as *Taiji* and *Qigong* to the medical community. When I describe him to people I say that in the bridge between East and West, Dr. Yang is the strongest plank!

At one of his seminars, Dr. Yang told a story about a man trapped in his house in the middle of a flood. In this story, as the water gets higher and higher, the man begins to pray for help…

The waters continue to rise and the man retreats to the second floor of his house. Just then another man with a canoe paddles by and calls, "Hop in; I'll bring you to shore!" The man politely declines saying, "I'm not worried, I'm praying for God to save me!"

As the water rises even higher, the man crawls onto his roof. A boat motors by, but he waves it off saying, "I'm fine, I'm praying to God and he'll save me."

Finally, the water forces him to the top of his chimney. A helicopter hovers over the house and the rescue crew lowers a rope. This time he waves off the helicopter yelling, "I'll be fine! My prayers will be answered and God will save me!"

Of course, the idiot drowned.

When he arrives at the proverbial Pearly Gates, God says to the man, "It wasn't your time; what are you doing here in heaven?" The man is overcome; "You let me drown! I prayed and prayed and prayed but you wouldn't save me!"

God scratches his beard and answers, "Look; I sent you a canoe, a boat and a helicopter..."

Throughout life you're likely to encounter some significant challenges. A positive attitude by and of itself provides no guarantee of success. A positive attitude is, however, an *essential tool* in building your success. A positive attitude is the foundation for positive action.

Who is going to ultimately be more successful, the person who embraces challenges and learns from failure, or the person who is afraid of challenges and avoids the pain of failure? Do your best to choose and seek out challenges that support your goals. Meaningful challenges increase your chance for success exponentially. Your positive attitude will fortify you as you face these challenges.

The point is that you can do an awful lot to control your own destiny. You can cultivate and develop personal power. You can apply your power to achieve your goals. You can share your power with others and enrich the world.

To accomplish all of this you may need to start by adjusting your perception of the opportunity around you. You've got to decide how to treat failure and how to accept success. You've got to constantly adjust your attitude to maintain a generally positive outlook.

You've got to constantly brainwash yourself!

In *Remember the Titans* Denzel Washington plays the coach of a football team facing enormous challenges during school integration in the 1960's. He's trying to inspire his players to rise above these outside conditions and distractions, over which they have little control, and come together as a team.

The coach shouts, ***"What's PAIN?"*** The team yells back ***"FRENCH BREAD!"***

That's the real secret. *"Pain"* is the French word for *bread.* Can you take some of your *pain,* slap some butter on it, and turn it into the bread of success?

I've left the element of fear for last...

I don't see fear as the enemy. In fact, fear is nature's way of making you aware of genuine danger. To succeed you've got to sometimes move toward whatever it is that scares you.

Some people define courage as the absence of fear. I disagree; *the absence of fear is stupidity.* Action in the face of fear is *courage.*

The problem is that our fear is sometimes way out of proportion to actual danger. When perceived fear is greater than actual danger, it's called *anxiety.* Anxiety can also be the fear of something that hasn't even occurred yet. It's very difficult to succeed when anxiety is preventing you from taking action.

Bravery is the conscious unwillingness to allow fear to dictate action. Heroes are those who weigh fear and act decisively, even when they're afraid.

The more *personal power* you develop the greater your capacity to face your fears. Power is developed by facing challenges and succeeding. Your success in turn develops your self-confidence. Self-confidence comes from the knowledge that you can succeed, and the knowledge that you can endure and even profit from failure.

Ultimately, you *will* succeed...

"Failure is not an option!"

Bunkai: The Application of Personal Power

The master and the student watch some of the senior students perform a choreographed set of movements called ***kata.***

Student: *Master, what are they doing?*
Master: *Kata.*
Student: *But what do all the movements mean? Is it just for exercise?*
Master: *It's a secret.*
Student: *A secret? What's the secret?*

The master calls two senior students over and tells one to do the kata and the other to attack. The attacker is continually defeated by the other student.

Student: *So! That's the secret!*
Master: *No, that's* ***bunkai.***
Student: *So what's the secret?*
Master: Practice!

Bunkai is a Japanese word that refers to the application of a martial arts technique or form. In martial arts we perform *kata:* sequences of choreographed movements, sometimes called the martial arts dances. Imagine what this martial artist would be doing if you could also see his imaginary opponent; that's *bunkai.*

Most of what we've talked about so far has focused on the development of personal power and why personal power is important in our lives. Once we develop personal power, what do we do with it? Let's talk about the bunkai of personal power.

As I started to accept the fact that I was the only one responsible for my own success, I became afraid, very afraid!

If I'm responsible for own success, I've got nobody to blame for any failures but myself.

In my life, this was an important and painful realization. I have experienced a great deal of failure and disappointment in life. I'm guessing many of you have as well. Like most people, there have been times in my life when I thought that nobody could possibly be worse off than me. In these times of darkness and despair, it was often very comforting to have someone else to blame for all my misery.

I've been laid off, I've been unemployed, and I've been in debt up to my eyeballs. I've been lonely and I've been alone. I've experienced poverty, illness and injury. I've been wronged by others. Can you relate?

I have to be honest; many times when my life was not going as I hoped, I found some comfort in blaming others. Failure wasn't usually my fault, it was my boss, the company, my parents, the school, the government, society; anyone but me.

Once I began to accept responsibility for my failures, I also started to accept responsibility for my success. From that moment on my scope of personal responsibility would include my successes *and* failures. I completely changed my perspective on failure. Over time I decided that if I owned my failures; I owned my successes too.

By accepting responsibility for my own success I opened the door to a very exciting process: the process of self-perfection. You might think this responsibility would cause me to fear failure even more, actually, quite the opposite. I started to realize that failure had a face, a familiar face that I could see the mirror every morning. I can deal with that guy!

The Chinese say that if you meet the devil on the road, shake hands with him! Once you accept responsibility for your own success and failure, you start to work with the one person with whom you have some influence and control: *You!*

I started to manage failure and adversity. I couldn't do anything about my company downsizing and laying me off; but I could do a great deal about getting myself started in a new direction. I could turn a disaster into an opportunity to create my own personal vision of success.

Through this process failures become lessons. When I lose money in business, I tell myself I'm *paying tuition.* When I occasionally have a lazy week I declare it an *unscheduled vacation.* If I really feel as if I should have done more, *I fire myself!* Of course, if I fire myself on Friday, I have to get myself on track so I can hire myself back by Monday morning.

Accepting responsibility for my own success and happiness is the single most important step I've ever taken toward shaping my life and dreams. As I accepted responsibility for my success, long before I had identified these concepts, I began to unconsciously apply the ***Dynamic Components of Personal Power*** and started to define my own success.

A note of caution: you may, like me, experience the great moment of enlightenment in which you accept responsibility for your success. That realization alone will not guarantee your success.

You've got to take action. You need to develop belief and faith. You've got to develop motivation and discipline. You need to practice balance, focus and timing. Nature doesn't work like some kind of metaphysical vending machine. It takes *time* and *work* to translate your positive thoughts and energy into the realization of your goals, ambitions and dreams.

Real magic happens once you accept responsibility for personal success; you begin to enjoy the process. After your enlightenment, that job you took just because you needed becomes part of your long-term plan for success; you may even enjoy it. You become more open, more aware of the opportunities and lessons all around you.

A little more magic happens at this point; success itself begins to take the proper perspective. Have you ever enjoyed a major triumph, only to find yourself disappointed in a few weeks or months? Maybe the new promotion, over time, revealed a lot of unanticipated responsibilities and hardships. A raise in pay that felt so good at the moment now seems like a high price for the aggravation. You may question your decision.

When success is enjoyed with the proper perspective, each small victory becomes a significant part of your larger vision of success. Any failure is accepted in its proper proportion, as just one small part of your overall program for success.

When you accept personal responsibility for success and failure you smooth out the highs and lows. The road is a little less bumpy. You enjoy the a lot more of the scenery along the way. Detours and delays become picnic stops.

Accept responsibility for your own personal success and the personal power you develop is entirely yours. Now you can determine your own *bunkai* for your power and define your own vision of success and happiness. So, exactly how do you apply this personal power and translate personal power into success and happiness?

It's time to refer back to the components of *time* and *timing.* You know by now that I enjoy old proverbs. Here's one that is truly timeless:

"The only thing that lasts forever is the present moment."

Think about this for a minute or two. If you really think about this for a period of two minutes, are you still thinking about it now? When you started to think about it, wasn't that *now? Well, it was, then!*

This concept is really difficult to express in words, but it's really not that hard to understand. The name we use for the moment in time we experience as the present is *"now."* It's always *now.* Now is when you shape your future. Now is the *only* time you *can* shape your future.

Too many people at too many times forget to take care of now. It's very easy to put off important tasks and plans and allow *now* to get cluttered with stuff that just isn't very important. Stephen Covey wrote an entire book on this subject titled *First Things First.* Go on our website and buy this book *right now!*

Take care of your *now.* What do you want to do with this present moment?

Physicists and ancient mystics may understand time as an illusion of sorts, but as average people, it's an illusion we have to live with. Time is how we organize the sequence of events that we experience as the progression of human life. Using the conventional measurement of time, we have only so many hours in a day. Use these precious hours efficiently and your power increases exponentially.

Apply the components of the *Power Triangle.* Start your day with some activity that creates a sense of *balance.* Start with some gentle exercise or meditation. Plan some time in your time for activities that bring harmony to your life. A simple example would be to make sure that even on a busy day, slot some time to work-out, and some time to spend with family or friends. How much on any given day is up to you. Balance applied in scheduling yields huge dividends.

You might have a career, for example, that keeps you on the road for extended periods of time. When you are home, it's important to apply the component of balance by spending more time with family and friends when you're physically present to them. I've known many people who have successfully applied this component to create a harmonious family life, despite spending a great deal of time away.

In order to apply the component of balance you need to plan your time. I'm not saying you shouldn't sometimes just enjoy life without a plan; but in order to have any *free-time,* most of your time will need to be scheduled. This is a great example of discipline creating more freedom. Busy people who carefully plan a schedule always have more free time than those who leave time to chance.

When you plan your schedule, apply the components of *focus* and *timing;* place each activity in its proper time when you can devote your full attention to the task at hand. You're always more effective when you plan to do brain work when your mind and body are fresh. Plan your brain work in the morning, or plan a workout before returning to intellectually taxing activities.

Discipline in scheduling allows you to focus better on the task at hand. You're always more effective and efficient when you can concentrate on the particular task or subject in the present moment. When you're distracted, your mind is scattered and work takes more time.

Schedule time for planning; including time for scheduling! Failure to schedule regular times for planning is one of the major reasons for failure in business and personal life. Your time is too precious to leave to chance. How often have you said, "I'll get to it when I get the time"? Most of the time, the time is now. If it's not time to actually do something important, it may be time to plan when you're going to do it.

Let's assume you've been nourishing your power sources of *body, mind* and *spirit.* You've been developing power through *motivation, discipline* and *time.* You've built up a reserve of potential power in the *material, emotional* and *spiritual* areas of your life. You're ready to apply your personal power through *balance, focus* and *timing.*

Like everything else in this philosophy, the application of your personal power is entirely up to you! I recommend spending some meaningful time thinking about this: How would you like to apply your personal power? What will your bunkai be?

Here are some steps I recommend:

1. **Evaluate your current talents and abilities.**
2. **Create a personal vision of ultimate success.**
3. **Design progressive goals.**
4. **Accept success with gratitude, learn from failures.**
5. **Evaluate again.**
6. **Make improvements and repeat this process.**

If you haven't already done so, create your own personal vision of your ultimate success. Where would you like to see yourself when you prepare to retire? What will your legacy be? *Write all this stuff down!*

Next, design a progressive series of goals and objectives focused on your ultimate vision of success. Set aside some time to reflect and reassess your goals at regular intervals. Traditionally, people took *vacations* to do just this! These days, a vacation can be more work than your job!

Continually evaluate where you are and where you want to go. Along the way you'll probably discover new opportunities you were never even aware of. As you do this work you develop new skills, you acquire new knowledge and vision; and your vision may change. Adapt your vision of success to reflect new knowledge, experience and opportunities.

Your personal vision of success and happiness is the canvas of your life. Your life is the painting. You're the painter.

To be honest, I never planned to be the founder of a martial arts system. The first real *ultimate vision of success* I developed was to make my living as a musician. As I seriously started to apply myself toward this goal, I discovered other opportunities.

In order to make a living as a musician, I had to acquire new skills and knowledge. I learned about running a business, moving equipment, scheduling, handling contracts, managing employees, and arranging travel.

As I was developing my music career, I took a job at a television station. I learned about audio and video production, performance, marketing, and advertising. As my band became more successful, I learned about handling publicity and speaking in public. I also learned the importance of polishing a presentation and putting on a professional show.

The skills and knowledge I developed to realize my original vision translated to new visions and goals. I can honestly say that everything I learned in my life as a musician has been instrumental in my other careers as a martial arts instructor, writer and speaker.

There are abundant opportunities to develop new skills and acquire new knowledge in every single day. Embrace abundance; nothing is ever lost or wasted: particularly your efforts. Knowledge, skill, material resources, fame and goodwill are transferable to new goals and opportunities.

Nature operates as a single universe, not as parts, but as the sum of its parts. Each of us is a reflection of nature as a whole. Everything I've done in the past is part of my present vision of success and happiness. Everything I'm doing now is part my future success and happiness. Everything I've done, and everything I'm going to do, is part of who I am right now. I can now see that every past experience in my life was prologue to where and who I am today.

As I said, your vision of success can and should evolve with the benefit of new knowledge and experience. With the benefit of hindsight I can now see that some of what I really wanted in the past was leading me away from success and happiness. Looking back, I'm now grateful that I didn't always get what I wanted; but I can now appreciate the fact that every detour in my life was full of valuable opportunities and experiences.

Somehow throughout this process I discovered the principles I'm sharing with you through the ***Dynamic Components of Personal Power.*** I didn't *invent* any of the components, *I found the components that worked,* gave them names, and diagramed them in a way I could work with.

Through the process of discovering these components, I became more aware of what they were and how they work. Sometimes I discovered a component by accident. Just like an astronomer accidentally discovering a new star when he's looking for a planet, I discovered most of the components only by trying to discover some other path to success. At other times I discovered a component only after reflecting for some time on a particular success or failure.

The most effective process of reflection is *gratitude.* When you take time to mindfully create a condition of gratitude, you'll discover exactly how you applied the components that led to a particular success. As you understand how you applied the components in the past, you gain greater control over your application of the components in the present moment. This is how you shape your future success.

Sometimes I found it appropriate to spend a little time with misery or depression, but I also learned to apply the ***Dynamic Components*** to change course toward a positive condition. I believe this is the process we call *healing.*

If you're currently in a depressed condition, refocus your mind and spirit on the process of healing. The mind/body sometimes creates a condition of illness, depression or disease to escape the causes of stress and negativity. That's fine, sometimes we need a break, but it's not healthy to stay that way for too long. Take some time to heal; then get on with the business of creating personal power.

Once you determine your vision of success and decide on some goals and objectives to realize your vision, then you can start to apply your personal power and access your reserves. You're now ready for the action phase.

When you understand your life as whole, rather than separate parts, you'll begin to appreciate life as a cycle rather than a straight line journey. You'll find comfort in the process of perfection. You won't feel disappointed in the knowledge that perfection will never be fully realized; you'll experience the present moment as perfect, since in this moment, you're fully engaged in the *process* of perfection.

When you express personal power through the process of self-perfection; you are already successful. Fully embrace the concept that everything you're doing right here and right now is part of your success.

Some time ago, I discovered an important truth as I struggled through a period of fear and self-doubt. I knew that I had to work on myself before I could be useful to anyone else. But, I also felt somewhat selfish, as I was spending most of my time focusing on my own issues and my own development.

I share the following thought with my students, and this phrase best communicates the purpose of martial arts study to those unfamiliar with the practice:

"The best thing you can do for others is to constantly improve your Self."

That little phrase very neatly sums up martial arts practice, and ***Dynamic Components,*** and nearly everything I'm involved in.

The primary application or Bunkai of personal power is constant self-improvement.

The secondary application is sharing personal power with others; in a word: giving.

Any other application is whatever you want it to be.

Why do I place self-improvement before giving? If you're not constantly developing yourself as a resource, what do you have to give to anyone else?

Giving is second not because it's less important, but only because you must first develop something worth giving. If you try to give what you don't have, you exist in a constant state of depletion. My experience teaches me that approaching life from a position of deficiency is exhausting; this is the condition of scarcity and poverty. The feelings associated with this condition are stress, resentment, fear and anxiety.

Develop yourself and your resources and give from a position of abundance and power. This kind of giving is true charity and kindness. You'll give freely because you see yourself as an inexhaustible resource.

But; earlier I said you have to *give* in order to *get*. This is true as well. This is a constant theme in my seminars for business people. You must give in order to get, but you can only give from what you have. Give what you have without any expectation of return, that's all. That's what *karma* is really all about; it's not a *quid pro quo* arrangement. Give freely, without any expectation of return, and the act of giving becomes in itself the most direct expression of power.

To access the power of giving, you need to also appreciate the importance of receiving. Most of all you need to gratefully accept the greatest gift in the universe. Every human being has already received this gift, but many do not recognize it *as* a gift. This gift is the most valuable commodity in the universe, but many people treat it as if it's the cheapest.

You know what I'm talking about? ***Life.***

The rarest and most valuable commodity in the universe is human life.

The unique combination of intelligence and physical qualities we know as human life does not, to the best of our knowledge, exist anywhere else in the universe. Study a little bit about the conditions necessary to generate and sustain life and you'll gain an appreciation for the incredible gift we all enjoy. Accept this gift of human life. Take some time to appreciate this gift. Actively give thanks for this gift; then return the favor.

How do you return the favor of the gift of life?

I've argued with some people who say there are no great prophets and philosophers in our age. Some say we've lost all our heroes. The fact is that we've never had so many heroes, philosophers and great thinkers and we've never had greater access to all of them. The great story tellers and sages are still with us, it's just that today we call them actors, writers, speakers, singers and comedians. One of our greatest works of contemporary philosophy is *Zorba the Greek* by Nikos Kazantzakis. Go on our website and buy it today!

Some years ago I was working at a television station. I was the disgruntled employee who didn't realize the great opportunities abundant around me every day. This was some time before I was willing to accept personal responsibility for my own success and happiness.

I was miserable, unhappy, and probably wasn't very good company at the time. Just to add to the excitement, my true love at the time decided to leave me, and my band was breaking up. Of course, based on my distorted perspective at the time, these were all conditions over which I had no control! I was in full *woe is me* mode.

My friend Nat came into the office one morning and tossed a battered, dog-eared copy of *Zorba* on my desk and said, "Read this, it will change your life."

I believe my response at the time was, *"Ya, sure."*

Read it, I did, and Nat was right. *Zorba* is an instruction manual for living. Zorba's greatest lesson was simply to accept and appreciate the greatest gift in the universe. If you want to pay back the gift of life: ***LIVE!*** "Why did God give us hands? *To grab!"*

If you want to show appreciation for the gift of life you've got to live life to the fullest. I won't spoil the story in case you haven't read the book. If you haven't, seriously, go get it; the movie is great as well.

Another great lesson about living life is found in the movie *Big Night* written by Stanley Tucci. In this movie two Italian brothers have recently arrived in America to open a restaurant. One of the characters in the movie is a competitor, Pascal, who appears to be acting as mentor to Secondo, one of the brothers. After refusing to loan Secondo some money, he begins pontificating on the importance of self-reliance and creating one's own success.

His advice?

"Take a bite out of the ass of life and- drag it to you!"

Life *is* abundance, but you're the one who has to sink your teeth into it and *"drag it to you!"*

There is an infinite supply of powerful philosophy available to help you stay positive or pick you up when the going gets tough. Go to the "Continual Education" section of our website; I regularly update the "Personal Power Library" and "Dashboard University" with books, videos and audio programs that are motivational, educational, inspirational, and some that are just plain fun.

Living life to the fullest is the best way to express your gratitude for the gift of life. The fullest expression of living is constant self-development and improvement.

Still, some people may confuse self-perfection with selfishness. Developing yourself is not a selfish act; it's the least selfish thing you can do. Your constant attention to self-perfection is the most natural and powerful contribution you can make to the world around you.

In my humble opinion…

The "Bukai" of Personal Power:

Embrace the process of self-perfection.

Ceaselessly develop your personal power.

Share your power with others.

Appreciate what you've got.

Live.

Poverty is Expensive

Have you ever been behind on bills? Have you ever worried about losing your home? Have you ever put everything you had into a business that just wasn't making it? Have you ever had to consider quitting what you love doing in order to take care of financial responsibilities?

Me too!

I've lived through more than one Maine winter trying to keep the furnace going five gallons at a time. I've chipped ice from my toilet when the oil ran out. I've been laid off. I've lived on unemployment in the middle of a recession. I've been turned down from jobs because I was "under-qualified." I've been turned down from jobs because I was "over-qualified." I've had good jobs, some of which I didn't appreciate at the time, and I've been stuck in lousy jobs.

I *can't* say I had to survive on just beans and rice; I preferred bean sandwiches! Some of my most valuable life lessons have come from my worst financial times. One of the most powerful lessons I've ever learned is this…

Poverty is expensive.

Have you ever bounced a check? How much does it cost when you bounce a check? As of this writing I know of banks that charge over $20 in overdraft fees. Let's say you're overdrawn on a check you wrote for $19 worth of groceries. You counted on getting a deposit in by the time the check cleared, but you just didn't make it. You just paid twice for your groceries.

How much does it cost to be late with a credit card payment? What happens to your 6.9% introductory interest rate when you're late the second or third time? How much do you have to pay to reinstate your car insurance or restart your mortgage? People who have enough money don't have these expenses; only people who *don't* have enough money have these expenses. ***Poverty is expensive.***

But wait, this is a book about abundance and positive thought and action. Why am I bothering to bring up this gloom and doom?

This chapter is personal. I assume that some of you, like me, have struggled financially. I also assume that some of you, like me, have struggled with the idea that accumulating power, particular financial power, is somehow selfish. Many of us were told that rich people are the great exploiters; that when someone gains, someone else loses.

Remember "Lie #5" from the first chapter? Every day people are told they don't deserve power, particularly financial power. They're told they're not good enough, smart enough, talented enough, or lucky enough.

Dr. Dennis Waitley masterfully counters these lies in "The Psychology of Winning":

"Success is not reserved for the talented. It is not in the high I.Q. Not in the gifted birth. Not in the best equipment. Not even in ability.

Success is almost entirely dependent upon drive, focus and persistence. The extra energy required to make an extra effort-try another approach-concentrate on the desired outcome-is the secret of winning."[27]

You have the right to pursue a life of abundance and wealth. The *opportunity* to succeed *is* your birthright.

I'm over my feelings of guilt about creating wealth. I'm fully dedicated to creating personal wealth and prosperity. I'm also fully committed to sharing my wealth with others, emotionally, spiritually, and materially. I'm committed to creating an emotional, spiritual and material legacy that will continue to benefit others long after I'm gone.

Create abundance and wealth in your life and you'll have more to share. Be a generous and compassionate person and your wealth becomes a powerful resource for your own benefit, and the benefit of others.

Part of my conversion is my own experience of material, emotional and spiritual poverty. I've made a conscious decision to create wealth. I *will not* accept poverty in any area of my life.

I'm sure that at least some of you are reading this book because you're absolutely sick of your current financial condition. Good! Let that be your motivation to create wealth.

Material poverty taxes emotional and spiritual resources as well. It's tough to stay positive when you don't have enough money. It's hard to keep the faith when circumstances seem to be keeping you down.

Some of you may have been born into poverty. You can't choose where you were born; you can choose where you want to go from here.

Some of you may have enjoyed some financial success but for some reason you were not able to keep it; you're not alone. Over 80% of lottery winners end up broke. If you made it once you can make it again; you've proven that!

Some of you may have made poor financial or business decisions. Your poverty may be self-imposed; *been there!* You always have the opportunity for a fresh start.

Some of you may be the genuine victims of circumstances beyond your control. Hurricanes, tornadoes, floods and fires happen, not much you can do about that, but you can choose to rebuild.

Some of you may be working 24/7 to keep your business alive. You may believe in your business and if you're like me, you'll probably pay everyone else before you take anything for yourself. Sometimes even great businesses fail. You may be experiencing the end of a market cycle. Big business may have suddenly become interested in competing with your small business. You may have run the family hardware store your entire life only to have a big box store come in and take your customers.

What about illness and injury? A serious injury or illness can wipe out your finances quickly no matter how prepared you might have been. I know: *been there!*

How depressing! What's all this bad news doing in a book about creating success and happiness? I'm not trying to depress anyone. I'm just trying to make a point: Whatever cheap bill of goods you were sold in the past, no matter what your current conditions, ***now*** is the time to move forward.

Everyone has talent. Everyone has ability. Each of us has some unique quality that distinguishes us from others. Everyone has luck. Most of all, everyone in our society has access to *opportunity.*

Some talents, abilities and skills are more marketable and more economically valuable at certain times and in certain places. Still, most everyone can, depending on your vision of success, become successful and happy through the expression of your talents and abilities.

I told you about the only two promises I will make to my martial arts students; these are the only promises I know I can keep. Both are contingent upon the student doing what it takes to get to *Black Belt:*

Within the scope of your talents and abilities, you'll have the capacity to do anything you want with your life.

You'll learn how to recognize and develop your talents and abilities.

Earning a *Black Belt* requires *motivation, discipline* and *time.* I discovered these components on my own journey to *Black Belt.* I've shared them with you as the components of the *Kung Fu Triangle.* The achievement of the *Black Belt* requires introspection, self-correction and perseverance; achievement through great effort: this is *Kung Fu.*

You can use this same process to find success and happiness in personal and business life. In this book I've shared everything I know, to date, about power; I'm learning more every day. I hope I've translated these ideas in such a way that you can apply the ***Dynamic Components of Personal Power*** to become a *Black Belt* in the *Art of Real Life.* Your talents and abilities form the foundation of your efforts.

How do you define wealth? How much is enough? Once again this is entirely up to you. Define how much wealth is enough in each area of *your* life. Define your *personal* vision of success.

Some people are very happy with very little money, particularly if they're experiencing life as they design it. Other people will remain in a state of poverty even after they achieve material wealth. If you make a lot of money, but still lack emotional and spiritual resources, you're still living in poverty; in my opinion, the worst kind!

In American society there is always some way to make money. Even in the worst conditions there are opportunities for financial gain. Millionaires were made while the Great Depression ravaged most of America. Every day someone once poor becomes rich; the *American Dream* is realized every single day.

Emotional and spiritual poverty are much more desperate conditions. To gain emotional and spiritual wealth your effort must come from the core of your human resources. Almost anyone can whether a period of financial scarcity, but nobody can live a happy life without some sense of self-awareness, self-worth, and connection with others. Becoming wealthy in the emotional and spiritual sense is hard work; it's also the most rewarding work you'll ever find!

Choose whether to generate wealth or to generate poverty; both conditions are self-perpetuating. Choose whether to embrace poverty or wealth; choose which condition you want to create in your life!

Emotional and spiritual poverty is even more expensive than material poverty. Depression, lack of purpose and deficient self-esteem are paid for in health and time; our most valuable resources.

So, what's the good news?

The good news is that there is no reason to accept poverty in any area of your life.

If you've been taught that only the lucky and the crooked get rich, you've been taught a bunch of crap! You can be happy as you work your way out of poverty; the work itself is a source of joy. Start by building emotional and spiritual wealth and material wealth becomes more accessible.

I've experienced a lot of challenges in my own life; I know it's sometimes hard to see the proverbial light at the end of the tunnel. Hell, sometimes it seems as if the whole tunnel is collapsing and you just can't run fast enough to get out! The fact is that as long as we're drawing breath we have options.

Poverty is *too* expensive. Work on developing personal power and putting it to work to create material, emotional and spiritual wealth. Then use your wealth to realize your personal vision of success and happiness.

Reject the inevitability of poverty and scarcity. Use your life to create and share abundance and wealth with the world.

As long as we're moving, we can move forward.

Recognize Abundance

It's sometimes difficult to recognize abundance, even when it's staring us in the face. Scarcity and poverty demand more attention. Scarcity and poverty automatically create acute feelings of pain, suffering and longing. We're wired to avoid or mitigate these feelings, so we pay attention. Abundance sometimes doesn't induce any profound or intense feeling.

Most people in Western society have a fairly high standard of living. Over 85% of Americans own cars, most families own more than one. Ninety-nine percent of Americans own televisions. Of course, that means that they also have electricity in their homes. We might complain about our cable TV reception, but at least we've got a TV and the electricity to run it. We might complain about the "Old Clunker" we drive to work, but at least we have wheels.

We're drowning in abundance. We're like fish in the water; the water is all around us but we don't even know we're swimming in it. Water, water everywhere but we're still thirsty!

There are people who, through no fault of their own, are trapped by *authentic* poverty. Most of us are not. For most of us poverty, is a matter of perception rather than a reality.

Nearly everyone in America has access to opportunity. As of 2007 there are no legal, institutional barriers to legal and legitimate opportunities. It is not legal to deny opportunities to any American because of race, ethnicity, gender, faith or in most cases and places, sexual orientation.

I'm not naïve; there is still prejudice, ignorance and discrimination in our society. We can all help alleviate these conditions by developing the power we need to oppose ignorance and prejudice through education and justice. Wherever positive people express more power, prejudice and ignorance wither on the vine.

I started this book by asking you to go and look in the mirror. If scarcity and poverty dominate your life I want you to go look in your mirror again; right now! Take a good hard look and ask yourself if you have the capacity to develop personal power and change the course of your life. Now ask yourself if you're willing to do the work, to do what it takes to improve your life from this moment forward.

If you answered yes to both questions, you've got everything you need to generate unlimited personal power. You've got everything you need to generate abundance and success. By the way, the *only* answer to both questions is ***yes.***

If you're already feeling pretty good about life, excellent! I hope this chapter will be validating, and I hope you'll share your abundance with others.

It takes practice to recognize abundance. The first step is gratitude.

Nearly every single morning I start the day by taking just a few minutes to consider all the blessings in my life. I think of the things I have, the home I live in, my friends, my family, my health, my talents and skills. For all the people, conditions and things in my life I simply say, ***Thank You.***

This simple ritual helps me start the day with abundance as my frame of reference. When I neglect my ritual I'm much more likely to feel scarcity and to think about what I don't have rather than what I do have. My *Gratitude Ritual* helps me appreciate the opportunities I've had in my life and keeps my mind and my heart open to the opportunities available to me today.

I've even developed the habit of giving thanks for trouble! Every noteworthy accomplishment in my life had its origin in adversity. In my study of success and personal development I've found that in most cases, adversity is a prerequisite for success.

Henry J. Kaiser, one of the world's most important industrialists once said,

"Trouble is only opportunity in work clothes."[28]

Count trouble and adversity among your blessings and you're well on the way to developing personal power, success and true happiness.

The vast majority of us could draft a reasonably long list of blessings right now if we just give it a little thought. Take just a few minutes and jot down anything and anyone you're thankful for. You can probably start in the room you're sitting in. If you're in a house with heat, that's a good start! If you've also got enough to eat you've got two-thirds of what a human being really *needs* to live a decent life.

Prayer is one of the oldest, and is probably still one of the best techniques to help us count our blessings.

I sometimes raise some neck hair by mentioning *prayer.* Some of you may consider yourselves atheists. Many of you no doubt have different religious perspectives than mine. It doesn't matter if you're religious person or not; if you've gotten this far in the book you must be a *spiritual* person to some degree, and I know you have at least some *faith* in the possibility of creating success in your life.

If you're not a religious person, don't get hung up on the word *prayer,* just practice giving thanks and focus your thoughts on your goals and objectives. Repeat these steps every morning. Call what you do meditation if you like. I use the words prayer and meditation interchangeably most of the time.

There are two basic types of *prayer:* prayer of *petition* and prayer of *gratitude.* The prayer of gratitude is where I recommend you start. Giving thanks helps you take inventory of all the resources you have available to you. The prayer of petition will help you focus on your goals and the future.

The process of prayer or meditation connects your mind and body with your spirit. Prayer and directed meditation are powerful spiritual actions that give direction to your physical actions. Prayer is a powerful technique for focusing your thoughts, and what you think about most intently is what you are most likely to manifest in your life.

If you have a personal relationship with God, then use it! Do you think God put you on earth to be miserable? There are some people who truly believe that; if you're one of them, stop wasting your time reading this book! The universe is the very definition of abundance. I cannot believe that God created the universe just to test our ability to avoid the enjoyment of everything he put here!

No, any tendency to accept scarcity as the norm developed out of desperation by people who had little control over their own lives. The acceptance of scarcity is always preached by those who fear losing power, to those with whom they didn't want to share that power. In our age there is no reason for any intelligent person not to recognize, appreciate and enjoy the great abundance all around us.

Poverty is not really caused by a lack of resources in the universe; it's usually a distribution problem. Sometimes it's difficult to connect the resources with those who need them the most. Only by developing our resources for compassion and sharing can we help those with the greatest need. Only those who *have* can share with those who *have not.*

Spend some time every day and be thankful for everything you have. During this time, don't worry about what you *don't* have, just be thankful for what you *do* have. If you're alive, you've got something to be thankful for!

One of the problems with what we call "developed" society is our obsession with comparing ourselves with others. I probably felt pretty good when I got my hi-def TV, but then I saw my friend's 45 inch plasma screen; now I want a 50 inch LCD-HDTV!

I think this desire for more material stuff is a vestige of our ancestry as hunter-gatherers. Most of us don't need to forage for fruits and berries or hunt our meat. I think there's something wired inside us that keeps us searching for more and stockpiling for the lean times. The extreme expression of this behavior becomes *consumerism.*

At any rate, I think it's important when I'm watching my modest TV, that I feel thankful for this window on the world and source of unlimited entertainment. I should be particularly thankful as I'm watching a hi-def documentary featuring the hardships of people starving halfway around the world!

I use television as an example for another reason. Have you ever scanned your cable or satellite programming for a few minutes only to say, "There's absolutely nothing on!"? The average cable system probably programs over 100 channels in basic packages. I may not find anything on that I'm particularly *interested* in watching, I may not think that anything available right now is worthwhile, but saying there is *nothing* on is just plain stupid! We have so much TV programming we're making ourselves physically sick on it.

I live in America. As I'm writing this book I live in the state of Maine, which by any standards is quite a nice place to live. I currently live in a modest home with my beautiful, wonderful and supportive wife; we have everything we could possibly need and most of what we want.

I do have ambitions to increase my material wealth, as well as a desire to constantly increase my spiritual and emotional wealth, but I have to admit that right now I'm feeling pretty fortunate. I have wonderful friends, I'm healthy, and I can do most anything I want within my means. Best of all, I have the opportunity and the desire to expand my means.

I have freedom. There are no institutional barriers restricting my opportunities. For this I'm extremely grateful; some of my ancestors weren't as fortunate!

No matter how much or how little you have in any of the areas we've talked about so far you've got choices. You can define your own personal vision of success. You can define what you consider wealth. You can decide what you want more of and how to get it.

You can create your own destiny, decide how you'll pursue opportunity; design and realize your personal vision of success.

That's Power!

Freedom: The Ultimate Success!

So what are you going to do with all your personal power? Of course you're going to use it to create abundant material, emotional and spiritual wealth! You'll then use this wealth for your benefit and the benefit of others…*I hope!*

Throughout this book I've said, again and again, that I am not the one who will define your personal success. A quick visit to the bathroom mirror and you'll come face to face with the only person who can define, design, and achieve your personal vision of success. Many people will help you along the way, but you need to accept full responsibility for the thoughts and actions that cultivate and direct your personal power for the results you expect and deserve.

Personal power is a tremendous responsibility!

Freedom's just another word for nothing left to lose?

When I was younger I thought this was a pretty cool philosophy; now I couldn't disagree more. From where I am today that lyric sounds depressing and self-defeating.

Freedom's just another word for choice. Develop personal power and you have more choices. You choose your goals, you define your own vision of success, you choose what resources you'll develop and access to achieve your success.

You choose your teachers. You choose who's going along with you on your journey to success. You choose the people you're going to meet, and the people who will benefit when you share your talents and abilities.

If freedom is *Yang;* the *Yin* is responsibility. I'm not here to lecture anyone on personal ethics; however, I will emphasize the point that *anyone* can develop tremendous personal power. Each person is free to express that power as he or she sees fit. My *hope* is that you express your personal power in a *positive* way. Express personal power positively with respect to yourself and others and life will be hopeful, loving, creative and satisfying.

Personal power expressed without responsibility becomes aggression, violence and selfishness. Power without responsibility is selfishness. Selfishness leads to fear, jealousy and resentment.

I truly believe that human nature tends toward the positive. It's our nature to share with others. We don't do well without the company of other human beings; we prefer to build cities rather than live as hermits.

Share your power freely and naturally. The most powerful gift you can share with others is yourself. Share your talents and abilities with the world. Help others become more powerful. As we become more aware of the great abundance of power available to all of us, it's much easier to share that power with others.

We can accomplish great things through sharing. When power is shared, our efforts are multiplied. Each single action creates ripples; these ripples become waves that shape the world.

If you become possessive with power you become selfish, territorial and protective. How can you possess power? You can *access* power, you can *develop* power, you can *manifest* power but can you really *possess* power?

Even the most tangible results of power are difficult to hang on to. Your dedicated application of power *will* produce measurable results. You can measure these results in the forms of *knowledge, fame, goodwill,* and if you wish, *money.*

However, because our time in human life is extremely limited, it is probably more accurate to say that we're just caretakers of knowledge, fame, goodwill and even money. The old adage is absolutely true: "You can't take it with you!" It's our responsibility to handle these resources with care and to do our best to leave increased wealth for the benefit of the next generation. Maybe the ultimate expression of generosity is that which we leave to the future.

There is no freedom in selfishness.

If you become protective of your personal power it is diminished. When you embrace abundance, there's no reason to protect your personal power, there's plenty for everyone. The very act of trying to protect power simply reduces the quantity of power available to you. Protect power and you can only utilize the power you can hold on to. How much is that?

Some of you may be saying "I worked hard for what I have; I shouldn't just give it away." In most cases I'd probably agree with you. Your time and your material resources do have a value in this world, and you have every right to expect fair consideration for the goods and services you produce through your efforts.

What you produce is the result of your development and application of your power. Share the power and your production increases exponentially.

Could Bill Gates run Microsoft all by himself? Very early in his career he understood that he could advance his goals and his personal vision of success much more effectively by sharing power. By sharing power he helped hundreds of other people become millionaires. Together, the people empowered by Bill Gates have generated billons of dollars that he is now donates to help thousands of people all over the world.

Of course Bill Gates does protect the goods and services produced through his application of power and the power of those who work with him. It would be naïve and irresponsible to do otherwise. Many people depend on the products and services created by Microsoft. In a free-market system this type of protection encourages innovation and creativity. How much creative energy are you willing to expend when you know the next guy can just step in steal what you've worked so hard to produce? Respect for personal property is essential for creative and material freedom.

Welfare states do not work; they encourage poverty. When you can share the material benefits of someone else's labor without the emotional and spiritual investments that created those benefits, you are sentenced to poverty. The human spirit does not develop through welfare; it develops through challenges. We develop the human spirit through creativity. The human spirit is motivated through challenge and competition. Welfare should be reserved for those with genuine need; it shouldn't be an entitlement program for those with the capability, but not the desire, to do the work.

Don't confuse competition with aggression and violence. Violence literally refers to an act of violation; exploiting and harming others. Violence is doing harm to another person without just cause.

When I'm doing my best and I beat you in fair competition, we both should benefit, shouldn't we? Let's turn it around and say you beat me. Let's say we compete in the same business; as my competitor you inspire me to learn more, perform better, and develop my full potential. Taken to another level, we might share resources, exchange intellectual capital and expand our markets through cooperation. Some of my direct competitors are also my most productive collaborators!

Without competition we stagnate. That's why we go to a great deal of trouble to prevent monopolies in our economy; monopolies destroy global innovation and progress. That's why so many Americans resist socialism in our society; extreme socialism destroys personal incentive and motivation.

Human beings crave competition. Competition feeds our spirit. Let's compete fairly and with respect for one another.

Fear of competition is another condition of spiritual scarcity. In my heart I know that if I'm doing my best, there is plenty to go around. This is the rule rather than the exception. Most of the successful people I've studied and met have faced some stiff competition. All of them say that competition helped drive them to succeed, or motivated them to seek new and sometimes greater opportunities.

We develop personal power through competition and challenge, and when it comes to personal power, there is always enough!

As you define your personal vision of success involve other people. Share the growth and development of your goals. Share the failures as well as the success. Failure shared is easier to bear and the lessons learned will benefit everyone involved. Choose these people carefully; choose the people who appreciate the opportunity and those who share your core values, goals and ethical principles.

Opportunity is the great equalizer. From its beginning American culture evolved to expand opportunity, not to guarantee results. The results are up to us and that's why we are, as a people, free. I don't ask you to define my vision of success, and it's not my obligation or privilege to define yours.

The only thing any of us are truly entitled to at birth is opportunity. Every great social and political change in our society was intended to extend opportunity to more people. Oceans of tears, sweat and blood were shed throughout our history to give people the opportunity to define and pursue personal success and happiness. Our founders created a nation of law to assure this opportunity.

It is our obligation to protect freedom and opportunity for one another. I *don't* have the right harm you in the pursuit of my success and the exercise of my freedom. When we are all respectful of one another, we all enjoy the benefits of freedom on a grander scale.

There is tremendous benefit in sharing your material, emotional and spiritual resources. First of all there are people who have genuine need for authentic charity. When we share ourselves through genuine acts of charity, we are acknowledging a part of ourselves in others. Any of us, through no fault, could at any time need assistance. All of us will someday be old and may not be able to provide for ourselves despite a lifetime of service. Sometimes there are circumstances and conditions beyond our control. That's when true charity should be extended, and *appreciated.* A true act of charity is a manner of expressing gratitude for the all the abundant resources in our lives.

On the other hand, there's nothing wrong with asking for and receiving help when we truly need it. When we accept the help and charity of others it's our responsibility to be appreciative. When we appreciate the goodwill extended to us, we're much more likely to act responsibly and return this goodwill when we have the opportunity. This makes for a very nice cycle, doesn't it?

However, we should not *expect* the goodwill and charity of others. We should not *expect* a direct return when we share our goodwill. These expectations cause emotional and spiritual poverty. When we *expect* something for nothing the whole world is full of nothing; we just want our share of it. When we *expect* gratitude for our charity, we can't help but feel disappointed when it's not forthcoming.

Lao Tzu said:

"Seek the approval of others and always be their servant."

You can apply this philosophy many ways. I think about these words nearly every day; to me, Lao Tzu is reminding me that the person I have to answer to in the end is *me. I'm* responsible for my success, *I'm* responsible for developing my personal power, and *I'm* responsible for expressing this power for my benefit and the benefit of others.

I'm the one in charge! I'm free! Personal power increases my freedom. Responsibility reminds me of the value of my freedom!

The ultimate benefit of developing personal power is freedom.

Freedom comes from taking action to express your personal power.

Freedom is the capacity to define your personal vision of success.

Freedom is the creation of your personal vision of success, and the enjoyment of those with whom you share your success.

Ultimately success is Freedom, and Freedom is the ultimate reward!

Your Time is NOW...Hajime!

What better time to start than right now?

Most of us can come up with several reasons not to start any particular endeavor, *right now.*

Everyone has the capacity to start moving toward success and happiness, *right now.* We all have the capacity to start developing personal power, *right now.*

Your goals and objectives are out there; your success is waiting for you. I'll once again quote the old Chinese proverb, it's a good one: "A journey of a thousand miles begins with the first step"...

It's time to get walkin'!

You may already be well on the way toward personal success and happiness. If so, this chapter should be validating, just enjoy it like a philosophical energy snack. If you're really feeling stuck, then use this advice as a philosophical kick in the ass!

Earlier we took a look at the expression "go with the flow." There is always a flow! The *flow* is going on all around us all the time. In fact, if you don't *go with the flow* you're likely to be swept downstream anyway.

The *flow* is the dynamic energy of the universe. This energy is infinite and inexhaustible.

You don't need to be an Einstein to understand that everything you experience is relative to who, what, where, and when you are. There are absolutely no boundaries on what you envision as your potential, and you don't need to check with anyone else to see if it's the right time to start realizing your potential.

So why not start right now?

One of the treasures of Chinese philosophy is this idea: "in stillness there is movement, and in movement there is stillness." This might sound pretty strange until you give it some thought.

Let's say for the sake of discussion that you've decided you want to become an entrepreneur. Let's make it really difficult and say that you've got no money and no credit. To make it even more interesting let's put you in one of the most difficult and dangerous businesses known to mankind; you want to open a restaurant!

I'm going to put you even deeper in the hole and say that although all your friends rave on about your culinary talents, you're not a trained chef and you don't know the first thing about running your own business. Many people, given this set of circumstances, would simply decide that opening a restaurant is impossible.

Bullshit!

I've decided that my life's mission is to convince you that you've got unlimited potential and can accomplish anything you wish, within the scope of your talents and abilities. If the idea of opening a restaurant has really ignited your passion, then let's get going.

"In stillness there is movement."

Want me to be nice, or honest? Assuming you chose honest, I'd have to agree with any rational person who would tell you that without money and knowledge you don't have the resources to open a restaurant *right now.* I'll also state that *right now* is the perfect time to get started.

Picture the surface of a great river. On a calm day it might not look as if the river is very powerful. However, *under the surface,* the current is inexorably scouring the riverbed, shaping the landscape, and carrying tons of sediment downstream to form farmlands and deltas. Just look at a satellite picture of Louisiana to appreciate this kind of power: much of present day Louisiana started in Ohio.

So you can't open the doors to your dream restaurant; *right now.* Be still. In our times this philosophy is more important than ever before because even with the scarcity of resources in our example, there are legions of predatory lenders who will gladly help you dig a big hole in the proverbial "mountain of debt" and set you on course for failure.

No, for now, you'll be still. But in this stillness there is movement. Just to keep this story short, suppose you consider your options for the best place to learn about the restaurant business? You could go to school; or you could take a job in a restaurant. Empires have been built by those willing to start as a busboy or dishwasher!

Learn everything you can learn. Meet everyone you can meet. Ask questions. I'm not talking you out of going to school for knowledge and information, however, where do you suppose all the knowledge and experience taught in our schools comes from? Doers often become the best teachers.

In Robert Kyosaki's book *Rich Dad, Poor Dad,* he teaches never to take a job for money; take a job to learn something. In the business world there are countless opportunities to learn at the feet of giants. Go to where the giants are! *Giants hang out at the Chamber of Commerce.*

In this little story you can work, start to put away money toward your dream, learn everything there is to know about the restaurant business, *and* get paid to learn and polish your skills.

After a couple of years you might decide that you're ready to strike out on your own. You now have the contacts, knowledge and experience to succeed. You might find out your boss is ready to open a new location, and you're the one who has been quietly preparing yourself to lead it!

Or, you might find out that the restaurant business isn't at all what you want to do! In this case you'll have exposed yourself to dozens or more different opportunities, you've acquired skills that will transfer to these opportunities and you'll have the power to redefine your vision of success.

The choice is obvious and the reward is the choice. Start now, today! Sit down and make a list of dream goals, then break them down into manageable goals and objectives. You'll find a couple of useful exercises at the end of the book to help you. Check out the resources featured on our web site; there are hundreds of great teachers who can help you through this process, often just for the price of a book or video program.

A martial arts competition sometimes starts with the cry of *hajime!* It's time to do battle! Go back to the first chapter of this book, look in the mirror and yell *"hajime!"* At the very least the yelling will put you in an energetic frame of mind. If you don't want your neighbors to think you're nuts, just yell in your mind, loudly!

What exactly *can* you start right now? This book is about the ***Dynamic Components of Personal Power.*** You can *always* engage yourself in the process of developing personal power. You can *always* cultivate and develop personal power and build your power reserves. You can *always* apply personal power toward specific tasks and goals.

You can constantly engage in the process of improving yourself toward the fulfillment of your personal vision of success.

Let's review…

Power is manifest by the three components of the *Power Triangle.* We produce power most effectively and efficiently when we direct our energy with *balance, focus* and *timing.* To some degree, you can apply these components in your thoughts and actions, *right now!*

Power originates from three sources diagramed in the *Energy Triangle.* These sources are *body, mind* and *spirit.* No matter the time, or who or where you are, you can seek out and participate in activities, or non-activities if you prefer, that will nourish the *body, mind* and *spirit.*

For the body, sometimes it's time to rest, sometimes it's time to exercise. Sometimes it's time to take action, sometimes it's time to heal. The mind needs activity to stay healthy and grow just like the body. The mind also needs rest and relaxation to heal and re-energize.

We constantly draw from and replenish these resources. As we do, we need to pay attention to the component of *balance.* We need to develop an awareness of when enough is enough, when too much is too much, and too little is too little.

Focus on the mind and the body enjoys benefits as well. Truly focus on the body in a healthful sense and the mind is nourished as well. This balance is natural. When we are not in balance it's obvious, *if we're paying attention!*

The way to keep these resources abundant is by nourishing the *spirit. Spirit* is the ultimate source of all our power. Only by developing our spirit can we access our full human potential. Only by respecting our spiritual connection to nature and others can we experience the feelings of happiness, love and contentment.

We access our power resources, and develop personal power, through the components of the *Kung Fu Triangle.* The *Kung Fu Triangle* represents the steady flow of life. When our action or work is in harmony with our true spirit in mind and body, we greatly improve the probability of success and happiness.

Right now you can develop *motivation.* All you need to do is look around you. Sometimes motivation will come from the desire to move above and beyond your current circumstances. Later, motivation comes from the desire to enjoy the feeling that comes with success.

Right now you can develop *discipline.* You can develop discipline in work and at play. You can discipline yourself to engage in the never-ending and enriching process of self-perfection. You discipline yourself through challenges; you can find new challenges *right now.*

Right now you can take your *time.* I don't mean this in the sense of waiting and allowing things to develop, though inaction *is* the sometimes the appropriate action. Sometimes you need to let the processes you've set in motion take their course. But I also mean that *it's your time; take it!* Take it and use it! Every single moment is a precious jewel that can never be replaced. We can produce many things; time we can only take.

You can develop personal power through *motivation and discipline* over *time,* and *your time is NOW!*

As you generate personal power through *motivation, discipline* and *time* you'll continue to nourish the sources of power in *body, mind* and *spirit.* You'll want to do this in a way that's beneficial, healthful and enjoyable. Life is action. Act with *balance, focus* and *timing.*

When your action is in balance and harmony you're action is self-sustaining. Balanced and harmonious action automatically replenishes body, mind and spirit. Balance in motivation, discipline and time produces harmony and happiness.

Focus on the here and now. When you're here and now, *be fully here and now!* Focus is attention. Pay attention, mindful of balance, and you'll avoid compulsion. Pay attention *with* body, mind and spirit and you'll always be motivated. Pay attention *to* body, mind and spirit and you'll always be disciplined.

Be mindful of the delicate balance and timing between you and others. When it's time to focus on you, focus on you; *the best thing you can do for others is to constantly improve your* ***self.*** When it's time to focus on others, focus on others! *The greatest gift you can give another person is your attention.*

Whenever possible, *go with the flow.* Sometimes you'll need to swim upstream, but know when; it can be exhausting! Sometimes you have to oppose some incredible forces, but know when; it can be expensive!

Wisdom is the result of experience. *Timing* is one of the benefits of wisdom. *Knowledge* can help you become aware of proper timing, but any seasoned fighter will tell you that good timing can only be developed in the ring. Timing comes from taking action, paying attention, and training with complete devotion to learning from both successes and failures, *over time!*

You can apply the ***Dynamic Components of Personal Power*** *right now!*

Right now is the time to take action. If you have nothing else, you have desire, and you have opportunity. The only other thing you need to get started is *time...*

...Your time is NOW!

Power Drills...

On the next several pages you'll find some exercises designed to help you apply the philosophy found in ***Dynamic Components of Personal Power.***

There are thousands of exercises and that can help you develop personal power and to apply that power for success in personal and professional life. If you find or develop interesting exercises or techniques, please let us know! Send your ideas by email to the addresses listed on ***www.JimBouchard.org.***

Stay up to date on ***Dynamic Components*** events, new publications, blogs, web audio and video programs and new resources by joining our mailing list. You'll find the "Join Our Mailing List" button on most pages of the web site.

One Big Goal...

In ***7 Habits of Highly Effective People,*** Steven Covey says "Start with the End in Mind." That's good advice!

Jack Canfield in ***The Success Principles*** identifies ***Principle 3*** as: "Decide What You Want."

To activate whatever it is that initiates all human activity you've got to start with an idea.

If you want big success, you've got to start with a big idea. Later on you might find that you need to take smaller steps before you get to your big idea, but for now just start with the big idea.

When you were a little kid, someone no doubt asked you, "What do you want to be when you grow up?"

You might have said you wanted to be an astronaut, a dentist or a giraffe. Small children aren't inhibited by reality!

Take a few minutes and return to that innocent perspective of childhood. Let your imagination work toward the one ***Big Idea*** that will charge your life with enthusiasm.

What's your Big Idea?

Morning Ritual

I've developed a morning ritual that helps me start the day with a positive attitude and the energy to take action.

1. **Gratitude:** I just start by finding several things to be thankful for and expressing my gratitude mindfully.

2. **Qigong:** I do a set of gentle *Qigong* or energy exercises. My preferred set is "The 8 Strands of Brocade." These stretching and breathing exercises help waken and invigorate mind and body. *This set and others is available on our **Energy Tapes: Basic Qigong** video. You can purchase a DVD or download version at **JimBouchard.org.***

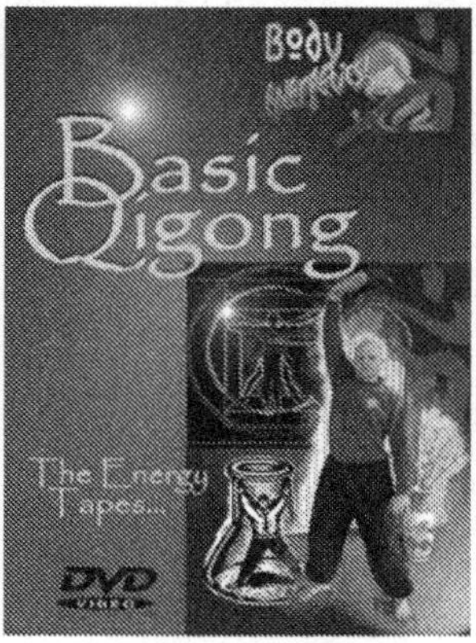

3. **Non-Directed Meditation:** I next take about 5 to 10 minutes to sit and breathe. I simply relax and let my mind settle without any directed thoughts.

4. **Review my Big Goals:** I have a page that I keep in a nice certificate folder. I update this page from time to time with my *Big Goals,* some positive affirmations and other items that help me focus my mind for the day ahead.

5. **Directed Meditation:** Based on my review, I meditate for another 5 to 10 minutes to focus myself on success for the rest of the day.

6. **Learning:** Finally, I spend about 20 to 30 minutes reading some material that will help me reach the goals and objectives now focused in my mind.

Coat of Arms

Here's an exercise for those of you who with an artistic flair, you can draw in the space below or use another paper. Use the computer and some clip art if that suits your style.

Create your own *Coat of Arms*. Include images and words that best describe who you are and who you want to be. You might include your own personal "motto."

My personal coat of arms is a penguin wearing a black belt kicking a football through a goal post. The motto says, *"Don't Dream It, Be It!"*

Meditation

There are plenty of great resources for meditation study and practice. You'll find books, videos and audio resources on ***JimBouchard.org.***

For those who just want a simple guide to get started, follow these instructions:

1. First, find someplace relatively quiet.

2. Find a comfortable position that allows you to breathe normally. Keep your back straight. If you're sitting in a chair, be sure not to slump. Lie down only if you don't mind falling asleep.

3. Begin to breathe normally. Let go of any stray thoughts as they occur. If you need some help letting go of thoughts, you might count slowly, or find a simple word or phrase to use as a ***mantra.*** Just repeat this word again and again in your mind until you don't even notice it. I sometimes use a Buddhist exercise where I say: "Breathing in, I'm aware that I'm breathing in. Breathing out, I'm aware that I'm breathing out."

Sit still, shut up, and breathe!

That's all there is to it.

Balance Worksheet

Deciding whether or not to take a particular action or establishing a particular goal *should* be a balancing act. You need to consider the long and short term benefits and costs in material, emotional and spiritual areas of your life.

Use this Worksheet to assess your goal or action.

Goal or Action: ______________________________

Key Life Areas	Yang (+)	Yin (-)

Powerful Resources

Over the past several years I've been obsessed with the search for the keys to success and happiness. In my heart I believe that we've been given this incredible gift of human life in order to enjoy the endless process of self-perfection.

During my search I've found some incredible resources. I've found valuable information and inspiration in all of these materials.

For a complete and up to date list of books, audio programs, videos and other great resources visit our website at JimBouchard.org!

- ✍ **THE POWER STORE**
- ✍ **CONTINUAL EDUCATION**
- ✍ **DASHBOARD UNIVERSITY**
- ✍ **PERSONAL POWER LIBRARY**
- ✍ **DCPP RADIO & DCPP-Web TV**

Visit www.JimBouchard.org!

Special Preview: Respect, Live It!

Taking Care of One Another

Excerpt from ***Respect, Live It! by Jim Bouchard***

I started my presentation as I had a hundred times, I simply asked, *"Can anyone tell me exactly what the word* ***Respect*** *means?"*

My prepared answer at the ready, I paused to let the question sink in. Would this group of first graders come up with something more insightful than *"Respect means being nice each other?"*, or *"Respect means listening to my teacher?"*

On this particular day I was presenting my ***Respect & Responsibility*** program to a first grade class at a local elementary school. This program was intended to introduce martial arts to local schools, and to show the public that martial arts are about much more than punching and kicking.

At that point in my career I'd been teaching martial arts to children for more than 10 years. I'd come to expect some remarkably insightful responses from kids of all ages. Today, I would receive an enlightened teaching from a first grade boy that would forever focus my personal philosophy and create a new mission in my life.

A hand went up; ***"Sensei",*** *the young master said as he stood up and bowed...*

"Respect means taking care of one another."

Have you ever heard a better definition?

I had to sit down. I'd been a fighter for a long time and I knew when I was over-matched. This seven year old kid had cut cleanly to the heart of the matter.

My prepared answer, by the way, was:

"To show esteem toward or demonstrate regard for someone or something of value in one's life."

What a bucket of crap! I'm not easily moved on an emotional level, but I've got to tell you that this young man had literally taken my breath away. I stood and bowed to him and told the class that his definition of *Respect* was the best I'd ever heard. I told myself that from now on, his definition would be the one I would teach and live by.

"To take care of one another."

Until that day I taught 5 rules in my martial arts center. They were good ones, but from that point forward I would only teach one. With this definition of *Respect,* what other rule would I need?

Our culture has lost sight of the *Rule of Respect.* We hardly use the word *Respect* anymore; disrespect has replaced it. Lack of *Respect* is ruining our society and crippling our political process. Our lack of *Respect* for one another is causing illness, violence and murder. Disrespect is costing American business an estimated 300 billion dollars a year.

It's time to reinstate the ***Rule of Respect.*** It's time to once again learn how to *take care of one another.*

Endnotes & References

[1] Cook, John, ed. The Book of Positive Quotations. Minneapolis: Fairview Press, 1996

[2] Cook, John, ed. The Book of Positive Quotations. Minneapolis: Fairview Press, 1996

[3] "power." *The American Heritage® Dictionary of the English Language, Fourth Edition.* Houghton Mifflin Company, 2004. 25 Nov. 2006. <Dictionary.com http://dictionary.reference.com/browse/power>

[4] Hill, Napoleon. Think and Grow Rich. New York: Penguin Group, 2003

[5] Dennis, Johnnie T. & Gary Moring. The Complete Idiots Guide to Physics. New York: Alpha Books, 2006

[6] "power." *The American Heritage® Dictionary of the English Language, Fourth Edition.* Houghton Mifflin Company, 2004. 25 Nov. 2006. <Dictionary.com http://dictionary.reference.com/browse/power>

[7] Cook, John, ed. The Book of Positive Quotations. Minneapolis: Fairview Press, 1996

[8] success. (n.d.). Dictionary.com Unabridged (v 1.0.1). Retrieved November 14, 2006, from Dictionary.com website: http://dictionary.reference.com/browse/success

[9] Stanley, Thomas J. The Millionaire Mind. Kansas City: Andrews McMeel Publishing, 2000, p 1

[10] Covey, Stephen R. The 7 Habits of Highly Effective People. New York: Fireside, 1990

[11] Benson, Herbert, M.D. The Relaxation Response. New York: Harpertorch, 2000

[12] Johnson, Steven. "Video Games." Discover magazine special edition: "The Brain, An Owner's Manual" Spring 2007: page 71

[13] Sun Tzu. The Art of War. trans. Ralph D. Sawyer. New York: Barnes & Noble Books, 1994

[14] Sun Tzu. The Art of War. trans. Ralph D. Sawyer. New York: Barnes & Noble Books, 1994

[15] BigGeorge.com. 2005. The Official Site of George Foreman. January 2007 <http://www.biggeorge.com/>

[16] Cook, John, ed. The Book of Positive Quotations. Minneapolis: Fairview Press, 1996

[17] Wing, R. L. The Tao of Power, A New Translation of the Tao Te Ching. New York: Doubleday, 1986

[18] Bryson, Bill. A Brief History of Nearly Everything. Danvers, MA: Broadway Books, 2004

[19] Reid, Daniel. The Complete Book of Chinese Health & Healing. Boston: Shambhala Publications, 1994

[20] Howard, Pierce J. The Owner's Manual for the Brain. Austin: Bard Press, 2006

[21] WinningWorkplaces.com. 2001-2007. Case Prospectus. Feb 2007 <http://www.winningworkplaces.com/>

[22] Wolf, Fred Alan, Ph.D. Mind Into Matter. Needham, MA: Moment Point Press, Inc., 2001

[23] http://www.every-thing.net/everything_ns/thought.html

[24] Howard, Pierce J. The Owner's Manual for the Brain. Austin: Bard Press, 2006

[25] Cook, John, ed. The Book of Positive Quotations. Minneapolis: Fairview Press, 1996

[26] Pearce, Frederick. From the Business Start Page. Feb 2007 <http://www.bspage.com>

[27] Waitley, Dr. Dennis. The Psychology of Winning. New York: Penguin Group, 1979

[28] Cook, John, ed. The Book of Positive Quotations. Minneapolis: Fairview Press, 1996

About the Author

In his life so far, Jim Bouchard has been a janitor, a carpenter, a pipe fitter, a firefighter, a professional musician, a semi-professional soccer player and an amateur boxer. He's been an audio technician, a disk jockey, a television producer, and a hot dog vendor with other occasional odd jobs thrown in.

He started his study of martial arts in 1985. Since that time he has remained active as a practitioner and teacher for more than 20 years.

In 1994 he started his first martial arts center and founded Northern Chi Martial Arts Centers in 1997. Jim is member of Cane Masters International Association under Grandmaster Mark Shuey. He is also the creator of the "Beifang Qi Taiji Cane" system. He is a 2004 Inductee to the U.S. Martial Arts Hall of Fame and has twice been featured in "Inside Kung Fu" magazine for his work with the cane.

Jim currently holds Northern Chi's highest rank of "Kansho". He serves as the Master Instructor to Northern Chi and is Master Instructor in Residence at the Coastal Center in Brunswick, Maine.

As of 2007 at age 46, Jim is still an active semi-pro football player with the Midcoast Chaos of the New England Football League.

Jim's philosophy draws on all his adventures and experiences. He is an exciting, inspirational and motivational speaker. His energy is infectious and inexhaustible. Audiences connect with Jim and his sincere desire to help everyone become powerful!

Jim is available to present Dynamic Components of Personal Power for your business, corporate and public events…

…Call 800-786-8502 or visit www.JimBouchard.org.

www.ingramcontent.com/pod-product-compliance
Lightning Source LLC
Chambersburg PA
CBHW031247090426
42742CB00007B/352
* 9 7 8 0 6 1 5 1 5 9 1 6 4 *